AF470064

Ancient Trees of the National Trust

Edward Parker and
Brian Muelaner

Ancient Trees
of the National Trust

SCALA

First published in 2016 by
National Trust
Heelis
Kemble Drive
Swindon SN2 2NA
www.nationaltrust.org.uk

in association with
Scala Arts & Heritage
Publishers Ltd
10 Lion Yard
Tremadoc Road
London SW4 7NQ, UK
www.scalapublishers.com

ISBN 978-1-85759-944-2

Project manager and copy editor: Linda Schofield
Designer: James Alexander of Jade Design
Printed in China

10 9 8 7 6 5 4 3 2 1

Front cover: A Scots pine (*Pinus sylvestris*) stretching out over Derwentwater on the outskirts of Keswick.
Back cover: Sunlight streaming through the branches of an ancient hornbeam pollard (*Carpinus betulus*) at Hatfield Forest.
Page 1: One of the many ancient ash trees (*Fraxinus excelsior*) at Kedleston, the hollowing trunks of which provide the habitats for a wide variety of epiphytic plants and invertebrate species.
Page 2: The remarkable ancient trunk of the 'Tea Party Oak' (*Quercus robur*) at Ickworth, which is believed to be at least 700 years old.
Page 6: One of the fabulous 400-year-old ancient sweet chestnut trees (*Castanea sativa*) that grace the parkland at Stourhead.

NOTES

Please refer to the Glossary for technical terms used throughout the book.

Historical periods mentioned in the book are dated as follows:

Mesolithic	9600–4000 BC
Neolithic	4000–2150 BC
Bronze Age	2150–800 BC
Iron Age	800 BC–AD 43
Middle Ages	AD 1050–1650

(Source: www.britishmuseum.org)

ACKNOWLEDGEMENTS

The National Trust gratefully acknowledges a generous bequest from the late Mr and Mrs Kenneth Levy that has supported the cost of preparing this publication.

Thanks are also due to Cadbury who provided significant funds to enable the National Trust to carry out its Ancient Tree training and surveys and to help with the production of this book.

The National Trust would like to express its gratitude to all its staff who have helped with the book, particularly Claire Forbes who has worked tirelessly to bring it to fruition, and Ray Hawes for his contribution to the text.

The Trust would also like to thank David Alderman at TROBI, Roger Clegg, Tom de Wit at Tolpuddle Martyrs' Museum, Ted Green, Tim Hills, Chris Knapton, David Lonsdale, Gary Marshall, John McCann, Sue Muelaner, Sarah Oldridge at Royal Botanic Gardens, Kew, Sir Richard and Lady Hyde Parker, Eppie Parker, Iain Parkinson, and Professor Donald Pigott.

Contents

4 Acknowledgements
7 Map of National Trust Properties with Significant Ancient Trees

8 **Introduction**
Brian Muelaner

18 **National Trust Properties**
Edward Parker

150 **The Future**
Brian Muelaner

152 Glossary
155 Bibliography
156 Picture Credits
157 Index

National Trust Properties with Significant Ancient Trees

Introduction

Discovering an ancient tree is a truly wonderful experience and the National Trust cares for more of these than any other owner in the United Kingdom. It is amazing to think that they have survived for many hundreds, sometimes thousands, of years mainly without our assistance. In an ideal world there would be no need for interference and trees would be allowed to go through their full natural life cycle, including collapse and eventual death, untouched by man and be replaced by others. While the sad reality is that these extremely important trees are threatened by an array of different factors and countless specimens have been lost, it is a miracle so many have survived. Mosaic Mapping recently compared the number of ancient trees on a range of National Trust properties over a ten-year period and identified that for a variety of reasons losses are still occurring.[1] Factors that are prematurely killing ancient trees include changes to agricultural practices, increased storm activity due to climate change, and the introduction of new pests and diseases into the UK through the huge plant trade.

A sweet chestnut tree (*Castanea sativa*) having its girth measured by National Trust staff on a recorder training course at Petworth House and Park.

Although tree management had always been a part of the Trust's countryside work, it was not until the early twenty-first century that it really recognised that it had such an internationally important collection of some of the world's most remarkable trees. But, even then, it did not know how many, where they were, what condition they were in or what threats they faced. For five years starting in 2009 National Trust training courses were run enabling around 700 members of staff and volunteers to record the girths and general condition of the trees in order to assess these amazing grand old specimens and then manage the environment around them. To date more than 34,000 have been recorded.

Trees have different strategies for the long-term survival of their particular species. Some, such as birch (*Betula pendula* and *B. pubescens*), are colonisers of bare land outside of existing woodland, their strategy being to disperse their prolific tiny seeds widely on the wind, which then grow rapidly with little concern for longevity. Birch wood is non-durable and susceptible to decay, so the species is considered ancient when only a couple of hundred years old. Rowan (*Sorbus aucuparia*) are also short-lived colonisers but they distribute their seeds by encouraging birds to eat their bright red berries, which encase a hard seed that passes through the bird.

The Old Man of Calke, an English oak (*Quercus*) in the grounds of Calke Abbey, is believed to be 1,200 years old and has grown down to form a squat small-crowned tree with exceptional character.

English oak (*Quercus robur)* as well as sweet chestnut (*Castania sativa*) and yew (*Taxus baccata*) trees can live to great ages and have a completely different strategy. They have developed toxic compounds stored in their dysfunctional heartwood that are designed to resist decay, and their wood structure is very strong so enabling them to withstand severe winds. This helps them survive for many hundreds of years, and in some cases more than a thousand.

The old adage 'over its lifetime the oak grows for 300 years, rests for 300 and slowly declines for 300' fairly accurately describes the phases in this much-loved tree's lifespan. The young oak is vigorous, growing quickly upwards and outwards to dominate its space and access maximum light. Once it reaches middle age, though steadily enlarging the girth of its trunk, its wide crown increases little. At around 600 years it begins to drop branches, the upper crown starts to die back and a smaller lower crown develops. It is thought that one reason for this is that the tree's vascular network is no longer able to support the vast upper crown. As the crown dies back, more light reaches the lower trunk and branches, stimulating dormant buds to grow, which form a crown further down. This results in a very squat tree with enormous character and exceptional biological importance, such as the 'Old Man of Calke' at Calke Abbey (see p. 42). Most long-lived trees go through this process, which is referred to as retrenchment, but at varying timescales depending on the species.

Early on in this process the heartwood begins to decay, eventually producing a hollow tree. This is a natural part of ageing and is in no way harmful; in fact it is beneficial to the tree. Heartwood is essential for providing the young tree with rigidity and its great weight creates a low centre of gravity, helping it to withstand the stresses from wind, keeping it upright and intact. Once the tree has a sufficiently wide girth

A sessile oak (*Quercus petraea)* at Lanhydrock with a bracket of the beefsteak fungus (*Fistulina hepatica*), growing through ivy (*Hedera*). This fungus produces red cubical rot, which converts the heartwood into brittle dry cubes that can be crushed easily in the hand.

The hollow in the trunk of the largest alder (*Alnus glutinosa*) in Britain by the shores of Coniston Water in Cumbria displays its aerial roots. These were stimulated to grow inside the tree when fungi began decaying the sound heartwood to absorb nutrients previously stored in non-living heartwood.

and a much lower more open crown, it no longer requires rigidity as it can now flex in storms; nor does it need significant weight to stay upright as it has a huge footprint and an extensive root system to keep it stable.

Additionally, all the nutrients that have accumulated over the centuries within the tree's dysfunctional heartwood are slowly released through the decay process. This stimulates the tree into developing aerial roots within its own hollowing belly, which re-absorb this newly available source of nourishment. Over the centuries the tree will have depleted the goodness in the soil and therefore this freeing up of the stored nutrients is vital for the tree's long-term health and survival.

As trees age they are more and more biologically important and an extraordinarily rich habitat slowly evolves: the temperate zone's biological equivalent of the tropical rainforest. The bark becomes more alkaline, suitable for very rare lichen species. Fungi cause the wood to decay, which is colonised by saproxylic invertebrates (dead-wood specialists) that munch their way through it. This hollowing process produces holes and niches for bats and other small mammals as well as roost and nest sites for birds.

Not only do many of the rarest lichens and dead-wood invertebrates require the particular conditions associated with exceptionally old trees, but they are also extremely poor dispersers. Some species appear to be incapable of moving further than a short distance from one host tree to the next. So it is crucial to have trees of a wide age range within an ancient tree habitat to allow such species to migrate from aged trees onto younger future ancient trees. Sadly, all too often there are few or no successors ready to replace any dying trees. Therefore, it is essential to keep our historic trees alive for as long as possible so as to allow immature trees sufficient time to develop ancient characteristics.

Some features of ancientness can be developed in juvenile trees by 'veteranisation'. A 'veteran tree' has characteristics of an ancient tree but at an earlier age, similar to a man going off to war and coming back a veteran, with missing limbs, possible shell shock or other battle scars. By tearing branches off healthy immature trees, removing bark on lower trunks or

Restored wood pasture at Croft Castle, which is one of the finest ancient tree properties within the National Trust's ownership. These magnificent oak trees (*Quercus*) are hundreds of years old and the site is an excellent example of what much of the British countryside would have looked like through the medieval period and up to the late 1700s.

The different stages of a coppice stool (above) and a pollard (below), in each case showing the trees just prior to being coppiced/pollarded, then shortly after work has been completed and finally with a year's regrowth.

repeatedly cutting off limbs, early decay processes are activated, in turn providing habitats for the saproxylic invertebrates. This is only a stopgap remedy, however; it is far better to maintain a resilient landscape with trees of all ages.

Ancient trees are also living archaeology, providing physical evidence of old land uses and medieval field patterns. The Trust rightly maintains and repairs its monuments, so it seems appropriate to do likewise for its trees. Some trees have even been participants in significant historic events, for example Newton's Apple Tree at Woolsthorpe Manor (see p. 148).

Wood pasture management

Wood pastures, vestiges of a land use dating back to at least the medieval period, are thought to have been formed directly from parts of the 'wildwood' that spread across much of northern Europe. It is now believed that this was not an unbroken dense woodland but rather a mosaic of open pasture, consisting of widely spaced as well as small clusters of trees, patches of scrub and large expanses of thick forest, continually evolving from one to the other through natural events, such as fire, fluctuations in herbivore populations, pests and diseases. Wood pastures were similar in structure with grass, scattered trees and scrub: ideal for use as royal hunting forests, where kings and queens together with their entourage could give chase to deer and wild boar at full gallop.

Commoners had a number of rights in relation to the land, including the important right of 'estover', whereby they were allowed to collect wood for fuel and for hand tools, carts and building repairs. The wood could be obtained by pollarding or coppicing. Pollarding is the practice of cutting branches that form the crowns of trees at about 2.5 metres above the ground, well beyond the reach of livestock and deer. The crowns then re-grow unaffected by the grazing animals below. Coppicing is similar to pollarding, but instead of cutting the trees above the grazing point, the area is temporarily fenced off from stock allowing the trees to be cut at ground level without their young shoots being eaten. Within both systems the trees are cut on a cycle of between three and 25 years depending on the species and the desired end product.

Historically, short cycles produced winter fodder for animals or fast-burning material to feed the bread ovens of nearby towns and cities (see Branscombe, p. 36), and the longer cycles provided building material, tool handles and firewood for heating. All were essential for the survival of commoners. Both systems were present in medieval hunting forests, as can be seen at Hatfield Forest in Essex, the most intact medieval forest in Europe (see p. 84).

At Borrowdale in Cumbria, the poles from pollards were used for constructing wattle hurdles to fence in sheep, an activity that can still be remembered by some of the older residents today. The harvest was known locally as 'stake and reis', from the Old Norse word *reis* – pronounced 'rice' – meaning twiggy foliage. To create hurdles the stakes were driven into the ground and the clippings woven between them. In the past the foliage was also cut and dried for winter feed for livestock, a type of farming that was still common in Scandinavia and northern Germany 50 years ago.

These agricultural systems generally went out of practice in the nineteenth century when access to cheap coal became widespread. Pollarding counter-intuitively helps prolong the life of many trees as it prevents the crowns from becoming sizeable enough to be affected by storms, so replicating the retrenchment process of ancient trees, but at a younger age. The repeated cutting also produces exposed wounds, which encourage decay to take place far earlier.

Wherever pollarding was discontinued, the trees grew increasingly large crowns causing many to tear apart. This was due to the weak union, where the branches were attached to hollow trunks, created by the repeated wounding through pollarding. The Trust and other organisations such as the Ancient Tree Forum (ATF) became concerned about the future of Britain's ancient pollards.[2] It was apparent that many of them needed their crowns reducing to prevent imminent risk of disintegration.

An ancient ash (*Fraxinus excelsior*) in Borrowdale, which has been pollarded on a five- to ten-year cycle over hundreds of years creating this short stumpy tree.

It is cut on a regular cycle of between five and 15 years, which produces a crown of lush, vigorous growth.

A lapsed hornbeam pollard (*Carpinus betulus*) at Hatfield Forest in Essex has been sensitively reduced by removing small sections of the upper limbs to prevent the tree from blowing over or tearing itself apart. This process will be repeated every five years or so, slowly reducing the height of the tree to a point at which it is thought to be stable.

These lapsed pollards had not been re-pollarded for at least 150 years and early efforts to rescue them resulted in unacceptable numbers dying from the shock of losing their crowns. The attempt to save these trees was actually inadvertently killing them. Over the past 20 years a lot has been learned. It is now known that it is crucial to phase incremental cuts over decades, gradually reducing the crown to a size that the tree can safely support. This management is very specialised and quite expensive, but absolutely crucial for the survival of these historic specimens.

The decline of pollarding often resulted in total abandonment of the wood pastures allowing them to revert to a closed forest woodland. Trees quickly seeded into the open grass areas around and beneath the ancient pollards. These young vigorous specimens grew up and eventually started to shade out the mature trees' crowns, causing them to die back. Left unmanaged, the pollards will die and be replaced by even-aged youthful trees. In these cases, the Trust carries out haloing, that is, the removal of all competing vegetation around the pollards. Again, in the early days people were keen to rapidly open up the trees from competition and to re-create the landscape of the historic wood pasture. Unfortunately this also proved fatal for many of the elderly trees, which had grown accustomed to living in a damp environment with little wind and limited transpiration.

The rapid change to the local microclimate put many of the old trees under stress and their roots were unable to supply sufficient moisture to keep up with the higher level of transpiration. There was now a greater risk of winds tearing the heavy limbs from the trunks inducing the trees to collapse. Even the extra sunlight on the trunks of some species led to a condition called sun scorch, which destroys the living cells in the thin zone immediately beneath the bark.

Wood pasture restoration in progress at Holt Forest. The area around the stunning ancient oaks (*Quercus*) has been opened up by removing the young trees that would eventually envelop the old ones, which are still visible in the background. Many ancient trees die due to competition from young vigorous specimens. Cattle will be introduced to graze the site to prevent such competition in future.

Over recent years the Trust has learned, through experience and research carried out by the ATF, that it is best to act quickly when trees are suffering from encroachment, but also to halo in gradual stages. In the first phase it is important to remove all competition growing through or in direct contact with the crown of the old tree and to create a small open space around the crown of between 2 and 5 metres depending on local conditions. About five years later the halo zone is extended by a further 5 metres and the young trees throughout the wood pasture are thinned out to allow an escalation in air flow. This process is repeated every five or so years and grazing is reintroduced to prevent further regeneration from taking place.

It is vital to identify trees that are suitable to become the ancient pollards of the future. These individuals are chosen while young for their deep healthy low crowns and managed by haloing to allow them to develop and maintain open crowns free of competition. To create a sustainable habitat, succession trees need to be of all ages, from seedlings through to ancients, so the process may take hundreds of years to achieve.

Designed landscapes

Many of the Trust's most important elderly tree collections now reside within designed parklands, although they may have originated within wood pastures or royal hunting forests. Famous designers such as Lancelot 'Capability' Brown and Humphry Repton were known to incorporate very old trees within their landscapes to create a sense of romanticism and antiquity. Indeed they even moved mature pollards to more prominent locations to enhance the effect.

Majestic ancient oak pollards (*Quercus*) within a historic wood pasture at Melford. These trees were essential for the survival of commoners up until the early eighteenth century, providing fuel, material for tools and construction, and acorns for pigs.

Although the trees are similar to those in historic wood pastures, many of the threats are quite different. Here the trees are within deer parks or grazed grassland. The main risks come from modern farming practices. Since the 1950s there has been pressure to produce more food on less land, achieved through the use of new breeds, fertilisers and pesticides. Unfortunately this increased productivity has had a hugely damaging effect on our special old trees.

Trees have an important symbiotic relationship with the mycorrhizal fungi that live, rarely seen, beneath the ground. These fungi sheath the trees' fine feeder rootlets that send out their mycelia and hyphae to absorb water and nutrients from the soil. They absorb the base elements from the soil very efficiently and produce a phenomenal network of delicate filaments. The fungi then pass surplus nutrients and water through the semi-porous rootlets into the tree and these are transported via the tree's vascular network up to its leaves. Trees, like all plants, have chlorophyll that allows them to photosynthesise, using the sun's energy to convert base elements into complex sugars, the building blocks for growth. The tree in turn transports surplus sugars and starches back to the mycorrhizal fungi, which are incapable of photosynthesis.

Higher numbers of larger, heavier cattle, sheep or deer compact the ground preventing rainwater from penetrating into the soil as well as reducing the available oxygen by squeezing soil into a dense solid mass. Surprisingly, sheep actually create the most compaction, their small narrow hooves producing the greatest pressure on the ground. When animals congregate under a tree in extreme weather, seeking shelter from rain or hot sun, they leave behind urine and dung, which increase the levels of phosphates and nitrates in the soil.

A dead oak (*Quercus*) within the park at Chirk with its replacement growing alongside. It is vital for the continuity of habitat that new trees are planted to become successors to the ancient specimens on which an incredible diversity of species depend.

The mutually beneficial symbiotic relationship is damaged by this combination of high concentrations of nutrients and compaction of the soil, which deprives the fungi of oxygen and water. Trust staff have been working to adopt more sympathetic land management, reducing stocking levels and removing winter grazing, which is the season when the most serious damage occurs. Fencing around vulnerable trees to exclude stock is also an option and the ideal area to be cordoned off is either a circumference around the tree of 5 metres past the outer branches or 15 times the diameter of the tree, whichever is the greater. This protects the soil where the tree's feeder roots are most concentrated.

While improving conditions for the existing trees to ensure they live as long as possible is important, it is also essential that future ancient trees are planted within these designed landscapes. All that is needed is for a tree or two to be planted every few years. Indeed, this is much better than suddenly planting hundreds of trees in a single season as it produces a good age distribution, which is much more resilient than a single-aged successor cohort.

The most suitable land management for the trees is a no input extensive regime using traditional breeds of cattle grazing on herb-rich pastures. This means no fertilisers or pesticides and smaller numbers of lighter stock per hectare, ideally grazing between April and the end of October. While this may sound like a less profitable way of farming, there are far lower overheads than with the more intensive methods. There are also agri-environmental grants available for farming in ways that improve the soil, increase the benefits to wildlife and prevent chemicals polluting water courses. Often the net profit is higher and the trees flourish.

An area of wood pasture restoration at Croft Castle.

Gardens

Several of the Trust's prominent gardens have ancient trees scattered around them, again some originating from old wood pasture or royal hunting forests. The Trust is world famous for the management of its gardens. While some historic practices have proven to be damaging to the mature trees, most gardens have adopted new ways of working that are beneficial. One such change relates to mowing. In the past, a very short-cut circle was mown around prominent trees to draw the visitor's eye to these beautiful features. However, repeated mowing of this sort occasionally harmed the tree's roots, actually cutting the tops off. Today, this system is being replaced by the planting of wild flowers in a circle beneath each special tree and mowing only once or twice a year. This stops root damage, is great for bees and butterflies, encourages earthworm activity which aerates the soil, decreases footfall which causes compaction, and lessens the gardeners' workload.

Another easily remedied problem is the positioning of seats. Historically, they were located beneath trees to provide much-valued shade for visitors on hot days. In your own garden having a bench underneath a tree is not a problem, but when the garden receives thousands of visitors a year it can cause significant compaction and erosion. It also requires more intense management of the tree for public safety. As the roots are damaged and the soil is compacted the tree reacts by crown dieback. It becomes less able to support a large crown so parts start to die; for safety reasons the dead wood has to be removed and some heavy limbs may need reducing. By moving the seat beneath a younger, more adaptable and less significant tree the problem is eliminated. Another option is to have mobile seats that can be relocated every week or two giving the ground time to recover.

It is also thought that a robust mycorrhizal community helps to protect trees from pathogens gaining access through the semi-porous root system. By reducing or eliminating the use of pesticides and fertilisers within gardens and retaining some dead-wood piles, the mycorrhizal fungi thrive and the garden is a healthier habitat as well as being environmentally friendly.

Occasionally it is deemed necessary to carry out work to ancient trees to avoid injuries from falling branches. This is always the last resort after considering various options such as adjusting the position of a path, moving a seat or planting shrubs or wild flowers to act as a barrier. When safety work is essential an arboricultural consultant with specialist ancient tree knowledge is brought in to give the best possible advice for both the protection of the public and the tree's well-being.

Within this book we aim to give a glimpse of the amazing wealth of magnificent trees in the National Trust's care, each with its own remarkable history. It has been a challenge to limit the number of trees to fit within these pages. We hope that the trees and their stories will entertain, educate and astonish but, more importantly, that you will be enticed to go out and find them, and to explore the properties in search of your own special trees.

1. A mapping consultancy company specialising in surveying ancient trees.
2. Lonsdale (ed.) 2014.

Overleaf: Sheep grazing close to the trunk of an ancient oak (*Quercus*) at Kedleston. The small pointed cloven hooves of sheep are more destructive to the roots of ancient trees than those of cattle or the feet of people.

National Trust Properties

Ankerwycke

Surrey

A copy of Magna Carta, 1215.

The Ankerwycke Yew (*Taxus baccata*), perhaps the oldest tree on National Trust land, is situated on the banks of the River Thames opposite Runnymede in Berkshire. On closer inspection, this beautiful tree with its vast fluted trunk is surprisingly colourful: its mottled bark is adorned with patches of pink, purple and turquoise. Although it has a girth of over 8 metres it is difficult to age accurately. This is because, as part of the tree's strategy for attaining longevity, it has become hollow thereby making it more flexible and resistant to winter storms, which can now howl right through it. Unfortunately the lack of timber in the centre of the trunk means that there is neither a complete sequence of tree rings to count nor any original ancient material to carbon date, two of the best ways of ageing a tree. Calculations based on the girth of other similar yew trees with known planting dates indicate it could be as much as 2,500 years old.

It is well documented that ancient trees have been held in high regard for thousands of years throughout Europe,[1] which is perhaps why the Ankerwycke Yew may have been selected as the site of one the most important events in British political history: the signing of Magna Carta (The Great Charter), which formed the basis of the constitutions of many other countries, including the USA.

Today, linguistic and geographical references demonstrate that the yew would have been an appropriate and suitably significant site for such a momentous occasion.[2] Magna Carta mentions that it was sealed between Staines and Windsor in Berkshire. This very much fits in with the position of the tree, which is now known to have stood on a small island in the middle of the Thames in the thirteenth century (the river has subsequently changed its course), offering a logical neutral zone for King John and the barons to meet. Also the second half of the tree's name – O/E *wycke* meaning 'wooded island' – gives credence to this. A twelfth-century Benedictine nunnery based on the island would have provided additional religious protection for the barons.

It is known that the Anglo-Saxons revered ancient trees and used them as sites for special meetings.[3] They believed that there was something solid, trustworthy and honourable about large trees, and that it was almost inconceivable that people could be untruthful while standing under such venerated ancients. Interestingly, the words 'trust' and 'truth' are believed to share the same linguistic root as 'tree'.

For many decades the Ankerwycke Yew was given little recognition, but since the celebration of the 800th anniversary of the sealing of Magna Carta in 2015, it has been considered one of the most significant heritage trees in Europe.

The distinctive fluted bole of the Ankerwycke Yew (*Taxus baccata*) under which Magna Carta may have been sealed.

The various stages of fashioning a yew (*Taxus baccata*) longbow using the interface between the heartwood and the external timber, which gives the bow both flexibility and strength.

Longbows and ancient British yews

Britain is home to around 90 per cent of all the ancient yew trees in Europe. Historically, yew trees were harvested to make one of the most effective weapons of war: the longbow. The Holmegaard elm bows, dated to around 9000 BC, are some of the oldest intact bows known and were found in peat bogs in the Holmegaard region of Denmark, but probably the most dramatic find in recent years was that of the 'Ice Man', whose body was exposed by a retreating snow field in the Austrian Alps in 1991. Among his possessions was a 5,300-year-old yew longbow measuring 183.4 centimetres, more than 20 centimetres taller than its owner.

From 1350 the demand in England for yew wood to fashion longbows began to outstrip the amount that could be supplied locally, resulting in much of the wood having to be imported. Such was the consternation about sufficiently equipping the nation's archers that from 1470 it became compulsory for ships returning to Britain to carry yew staves. King Richard III ordered ten staves for every barrel of wine imported, but within 30 years of this decree concerns were being raised about the annihilation of Europe's yew forests and there were calls for a total ban on cutting yew trees in parts of Austria and Bavaria. By the mid-sixteenth century wholesale felling of yews regardless of age and condition was taking place throughout Europe except for in Britain. British yew timber was considered inferior and escaped drastic felling and this, along with the absence of major land-based wars over the last 500 years and the sanctity of yew trees growing in churchyards, is believed to be the reason for Britain's remarkable collection of ancient yew trees today.

1. Hageneder 2007.
2. Ibid.
3. Hooke 2010.

Ashridge Estate
Hertfordshire

The Ashridge Estate's mosaic of woodland and downland habitats straddles the Chiltern Hills. At its core are Frithsden Woods, breathtaking at any time of the year, and home to some enormous beech trees (*Fagus sylvatica*), many of which are over 25 metres tall and have girths in excess of 8 metres. In April and May these giant pollards tower over great swathes of bluebells; in autumn the woods are aflame with orange and yellow leaves, while in winter their huge smooth limbs create magnificent silhouettes against menacing skies.

One of the largest beeches rose to fame as the 'Whomping Willow' located in the grounds of Hogwarts School of Witchcraft and Wizardry in the *Harry Potter* films (2001–11). It also appeared in *Robin Hood: Prince of Thieves* (1991). Sadly, age finally caught up with it and in June 2014 it collapsed. Today, its vast trunk and colossal branches – grey and elephantine – lie among the leaf litter on the forest floor. This gentle giant may have been more than 600 years old and is now making its final contribution to the ancient woodland by providing microhabitats for many species of fungi and invertebrates as it slowly decomposes.

Beech nuts for human food and pannage

For thousands of years beeches have been an essential source of food. The tri-lobed nuts in their prickly seed cases are highly nutritious and rich in protein and oil. Similar to the sweet chestnuts (*Castanea sativa*) in Mediterranean regions, they were once vital to man's survival over the lean winter months. As agriculture developed and food supplies became more reliable the role of the beech nut in human diets became less important.

Beech nuts were also essential for feeding swine. The practice of releasing domestic pigs into woodlands so that they could forage on beech nuts as well as chestnuts and acorns for a limited number of days a year was referred to as 'pannage'. The system, dating back to the Iron Age, started to die out in the Middle Ages and dramatically declined following the Enclosure Acts from the 1750s onwards. Today the only location where pannage is still carried out is in the New Forest, Hampshire. The right of pannage was granted to commoners to let their pigs graze on common land or royal land for up to

The distinctive smooth bark of an ancient beech tree (*Fagus sylvatica*), several hundred years old, which rises up into a wintery sky at Frithsden Woods on the Ashridge Estate.

An inscription made by American servicemen, just before they left to take part in the D-Day landings, is still visible on one of the old beech trees (*Fagus sylvatica*).

60 days a year and for which there was usually a charge or 'agistment'. According to the Charter of the Forest (1217), pannage was given by permission of the forest justices, at one or two pence per pig. Pannage pigs were required to be ringed to reduce the damage they might cause to the forest floor. The word pannage is Late Middle English from the O/F *pasnage*, derived from Medieval Latin *pascere*, 'to feed'.

Beech trees and graffiti

A short distance from the National Trust's office at Ashridge stands a group of magnificent yet mostly time-weary beech trees, many of which are likely to be over 300 years old. While some have snapped off halfway up their trunks and others display jagged stumps where limbs have been ripped off by storms, there are a number that are still straight-trunked and vigorous, despite their great age.

One of the distinctive features of a large beech tree is its smooth, soft bark. Blemish free, it is the preferred canvas for graffiti artists. While newly carved graffiti may be considered to be vandalism, on many of the ancient trees, such as the great 'Harry Potter' beech that recently fell down at Ashridge, there is evidence of inscriptions that may be hundreds of years old and which are now regarded as historical documents in their own right. Just as graffiti by the artist Banksy is valued as art, so too can tree graffiti. A sobering piece of historic graffiti can be seen on a 300-year-old beech tree close to the Trust office. It was created by a group of young American GIs who knew that they would soon be going to the beaches of Normandy; the carving is dated 4 May 1944, just weeks before D-Day. Was it bravado or fear that drove them to write the initials of their eight home states, from South Dakota in the mid-west to Texas in the far south?

The ancient beech tree (*Fagus sylvatica*) that featured in the *Harry Potter* and *Robin Hood: Prince of Thieves* films has recently fallen and has begun to be colonised by fungi and many types of specialist invertebrates.

In late afternoon sunlight, the brightly coloured autumn leaves are spectacular.

Blickling

Norfolk

Blickling is famous for its fine red-brick house built between 1616 and 1624 by Robert Lyminge, and as the former mansion in which Anne Boleyn was believed to have been born. Today the house has a grand entrance lined with elegant ancient yew hedges and is set in spectacular landscaped gardens. Beyond the formality of the gardens, the woodland and parkland contain some of Blickling's finest ancient and veteran oak, ash, beech and lime trees.

Blickling Hall from the west.

The wood pasture that extends around the central garden at Blickling is where many of the oldest and largest trees are found.

The profusion of plants, including yellow archangel (*Lamium galeobdolon*), dog's mercury (*Mercurialis perennis*) and the great drifts of bluebells (*Hyacinthoides non-scripta*), form a carpet during the early spring, indicating that the Great Wood is ancient woodland.

Walking lime trees

Ancient small-leaved limes (*Tilia cordata*) also grow in the Great Wood and one is in the process of 'walking', albeit at glacial speed. The trees are considered to be a relic of the mythical wildwood that once covered north-west Europe. They are true natives of British woodland but since the climate changed around 4,500 years ago they have become inefficient at reproduction by means of flowers and seeds. Therefore, many of the small-leaved limes in Britain today have grown by generating suckers from branches that have dipped down and taken root in the soil a short distance from the main trunk.

A tree on the edge of the Great Wood demonstrates this perfectly. Over centuries a number of the large lateral

An ancient 'walking' small-leaved lime (*Tilia cordata*) on the edge of the Great Wood.

branches have touched the floor and rooted. After decades the umbilical-like connection between the 'mother' tree and the young tree disappears and the new tree becomes fully independent. This process can happen numerous times allowing a tree to theoretically move across the landscape, eventually leading to the growth of groves of genetically identical trees. This gives rise to an interesting question: how old are the magnificent lime trees that stand on the medieval wood banks at Blickling? Each of the huge limes in the Great Wood is believed to be over 600 years old. However, it could be argued that if they are actually genetically identical to trees that flourished 3,000 to 4,000 years ago, they could also be identical to individuals that were alive during the Neolithic period, around 8,000 years ago.

Borrowdale
Cumbria

The 'Fraternal Four'

Borrowdale is a steep-sided glacial valley that winds for around 11 kilometres (7 miles) from the town of Keswick up to the Honister Pass. Beyond Derwentwater, resplendent with alder trees (*Alnus*) that fringe its deep blue waters, it divides into three distinct valleys: Watendlath, Stonethwaite and Seathwaite. Perched high on a sheer slope, halfway along the Seathwaite Valley, grow some of Britain's most famous and much-loved yew trees (*Taxus baccata*). William Wordsworth, struck by their great age and decaying beauty, wrote his famous poem 'Yew Trees' in 1803; since then they have been known as the 'Fraternal Four'.

> There is a Yew-tree, pride of Lorton Vale,
> Which to this day stands single, in the midst
> Of its own darkness, as it stood of yore:
> Not loathe to furnish weapons for the Bands
> Of Umfraville or Percy ere they marched
> To Scotland's heaths; or those that crossed the sea
> And drew their sounding bows at Azincour,
> Perhaps at earlier Crecy, or Poictiers.
> Of vast circumference and gloom profound
> This solitary Tree! – a living thing
> Produced too slowly ever to decay;
> Of form and aspect too magnificent
> To be destroyed. But worthier still of note
> Are those fraternal Four of Borrowdale,
> Joined in one solemn and capacious grove;
> Huge trunks! – and each particular trunk a growth
> Of intertwisted fibres serpentine
> Up-coiling and inveterately convolved.[1]

Today the trees resemble battle-weary war veterans. One lies on its side, mortally wounded, while shredded branches from the remaining three, wrenched violently off their stout trunks by gales, carpet the ground. But this is not recent damage; it is the aftermath of the great storm of 1883. Yew trees operate on a timescale so different from our own that during the longest of human lifetimes they seem to remain virtually unaltered: a constant in an evolving landscape, almost immortal. Surprisingly, it is likely that these trees are moving forward, repairing and regenerating, but in tree time.

The Fraternal Four yew trees (*Taxus baccata*) are quite distinct from one another in both shape and in the colour of their bark.

Overleaf: The damage to the Fraternal Four (*Taxus baccata*) from the great storm of 1883 is still visible today more than 130 years later.

Looking from near Stonethwaite into Borrowdale, the many ancient ash pollards (*Fraxinus excelsior*) are resplendent in the valley.

A group of ancient trees known locally as 'cropping ashes' (*Fraxinus excelsior*).

Originally, the four trees were magnificent specimens and were described as being near the Seatoller Bridge in *Sylvan's Pictorial Handbook*: 'near this spot may be seen the Borrowdale Yews among the copse-wood: there are four large trees, and some smaller ones; the finest measuring seven yards in circumference [at 4 feet from the ground], and, although exceedingly old, is not yet decayed.'[2]

A few years later, after the storm had ravaged the yews, John Lowe visited and documented them as part of the first systematic study of old yews in Britain and Ireland. In his book *The Yew Trees of Great Britain and Ireland*, he writes: 'But in the great gale of 1883 one of them was uprooted; leading branches of the others were wrenched from the main stem, and although three still remain, the solemn majesty of the grove is gone.'[3]

Finding the best way to support the yews continues. The National Trust recently had material from each tree DNA tested and the results proved that two of the huge trees are actually one, being genetically identical and originally from the same tree: the 'Fraternal Three-and-a-half' perhaps!

The ancient cropping ashes

A prolific tree, and one that best represents the ancient management of the valleys of Borrowdale over the centuries, is the ash (*Fraxinus excelsior*). Probably the most abundant native species in Cumbria, it grows equally well in the open or in a hedgerow. It is easily recognisable, even from a distance, with its pale bark and candelabra-like branches, which droop down but ascend at the tips.

From any view looking over the valleys of Borrowdale it is possible to see what are locally referred to as 'cropping ashes': trees that have been pollarded every few years, primarily for poles. These poles, in addition to providing material for firewood and for tool handles, were employed in making wattle hurdles to fence in sheep.

The harvest of poles and foliage from ash pollards (*Fraxinus excelsior*) once provided fuel, fencing material and fodder for livestock.

The National Trust is careful to maintain the system of pollarding not only for its aesthetic but also for the wellbeing of the trees. Many trees, such as ash, beech (*Fagus sylvatica*) and lime (*Tilia*), achieve a far greater age than is possible in natural circumstances when they are coppiced or pollarded. Despite their small stature, the ash of Borrowdale may be many centuries old, thanks to the combination of harsh growing conditions and the practice of pollarding. The more frequently a tree is pollarded the slower its trunk increases in size, since it has to put all of its resources into growing a new crown to enable photosynthesis to take place.

In 1772, the traveller and naturalist Thomas Pennant wrote in *A Tour in Scotland 1769 and a Voyage to the Hebrides* about ash pollards and the impact of competition for wood on the Lake District farmers and smelters:

> Observe that the tops of the ash trees were lopped; and was informed that it was done to feed the cattle in the autumn when the grass was in decline; the cattle peeling off the bark as food. In Queen Elizabeth's time the inhabitants of Colton and Hawkshead fells remonstrated against the number of forges in the county, because they consumed all the loppings and croppings, the sole winter food for their cattle.[4]

Today, looking out over the sweeping beauty of the valleys of Borrowdale and beyond, it is hard to imagine that iron smelting, charcoal burning, and copper and graphite mining were once carried out here. The area under the ownership of the National Trust around Keswick extends to 29,173 hectares, comprising 11 farms, half of Derwentwater (including the main islands) and a number of hamlets such as Seathwaite as well as the Trust's first acquisition in the Lake District, Brandlehow Woods, which was purchased in 1902.

1. Extract from 'Yew Trees', Wordsworth 1994, p. 185.
2. Sylvan 1847.
3. Lowe 1897.
4. Pennant 1772, p. 33.

Box Hill

Surrey

Box Hill has long been renowned as an idyllic picnicking area for Londoners; it became particularly popular with the advent of trains and bicycles. The Hill takes its name from the many box trees (*Buxus sempervirens*) that grow in among the beech- (*Fagus sylvatica*) and yew- (*Taxus baccata*) dominated woodland on this part of the North Downs. It is also famously associated with Jane Austen's book *Emma* (1815). Even as early as August 1655 John Evelyn wrote of Box Hill, 'There were such goodly walks and hills shaded with yews as render the place extremely agreeable'.[1]

The Hill is home to a remarkable large-leaved lime tree (*Tilia platyphyllos*). Located close to the stepping stones across the River Mole at the base of the great chalk escarpment it has a girth of well over 8 metres. It is almost certainly one of the earliest examples of this species of lime ever recorded in the United Kingdom. Botanist Christopher Merrett collected his specimens from the foot of Box Hill.[2] Now over 400 years old, the tree was fully mature and recorded for scientific posterity in 1666, the year of the Great Fire of London.

Due to its scarcity, of all of Britain's native forest trees it is only the large-leaved lime that is included in the *British Red Data Book*. It has a preference for growing on steep, well-drained limestone or chalk escarpments, similar to those at Box Hill, and is especially rare in southern Britain.

In addition to having many wild box trees (*Buxus sempervirens*), Box Hill has a number of groves of ancient yews (*Taxus baccata*).

The expansive views across the woodland have been a major attraction for Londoners for more than 200 years.

The North Downs, which run from the White Cliffs of Dover into Hampshire, were formed from a prehistoric sea bed. Millions of years ago the skeletons of microscopic organisms settled onto what was then the Atlantic Ocean floor when their lives had ended. The calcareous sediment became compressed under the weight of the sea creating chalk and limestone until geological activity lifted the deposit high above present-day sea levels. Without this material the large-leafed lime trees would have been unable to thrive.

The importance of limes in prehistoric and historic times

Limes were important to the ancient peoples of Europe, particularly during the Mesolithic and Neolithic periods. This is because, located just under the bark, is a fibrous layer (known as bast) from which they could make rope by soaking the fibres in water and twisting them together. The rope was strong enough to be used for moving the vast stones at Stonehenge or for making rope bridges. The lime fibres also provided material for clothing.

While walking in the Ötztal area of the Austrian Alps in 1991, two hikers made a grim discovery of a frozen body. Archaeology revealed it was the oldest frozen mummified body ever found and was named Özi the 'Ice Man', who had perished around 5,300 years ago. His 13-centimetre-long dagger had a lime-wood handle and was kept in a triangular 12-centimetre-long sheath-like scabbard consisting of a mesh of tree bast. A net that was probably used for catching small birds and animals was fashioned from tree-bast string.

Much more recently but still almost two millennia ago, Severa, the wife of a Roman officer, Aelius Brochus, wrote to her friend Sulpicia Lepidina inviting her to come to celebrate her birthday. This is the oldest surviving record in which we can hear the words of an ordinary person and it was made on limewood tablets that were preserved in a soggy patch of ground at the Roman fort of Vindolanda, just south of the future Hadrian's Wall.[3]

For many centuries lime has been the favoured material for sculptures as it possesses a very fine grain and is lightweight, making it ideal for delicate detailed carving. It is also a popular wood for electric guitars due to its good acoustic qualities.

1. See Evelyn 1850.
2. Merrett 1666.
3. Miles 2006, p. 120.

The large-leaved lime (*Tilia platyphyllos*) recorded by botanist Christopher Merrett in 1666 stands at the foot of Box Hill.

Branscombe

Devon

One of the ancient ash pollards (*Fraxinus excelsior*) that stand on the steep slopes above Branscombe village and which have provided fuel wood for hundreds of years.

In the village of Branscombe it is still possible to experience a small slice of history while enjoying cake and a cup of coffee in the old bakery. Until relatively recently the building housed the last traditional working village bakery in Devon, which had produced bread for the local people for several centuries. The fuel for the ovens came in the form of ash faggots sustainably harvested from a scattered forest of ancient ash trees (*Fraxinus excelsior*) that grew on the steep-sided hills behind the village. Sadly, the closure of the bakery in 1987 marked the end of this system of growing and harvesting firewood in Branscombe. However, the ash trees persist and are managed by the National Trust.

The trees have adapted to centuries of being cut for poles to fire the bread ovens, and have developed swollen tops to their trunks that give the appearance of clenched fists. The naturalist writer, Roger Deakin, believed they should be celebrated as organic monuments to centuries of expert woodmanship and also to a system that once provided fuel, timber and livelihoods to great numbers of people across Britain.[1]

Members of the Collier family at Branscombe bakery. The ash (*Fraxinus excelsior*) faggots to fuel the ovens can be seen under the table.

Wood hay

The twigs and leaves of ash trees were long collected for use as 'wood hay' for animal feed during winter in areas where 'grass hay' was difficult to produce. Ash is second only to elm foliage (*Ulmus*) as a leaf fodder that is rich in nutrients and soft enough for the cattle and sheep to chew. The lack of ash and other tree fodder in animal diets today results in farmers having to use chemical supplements in order to maintain healthy, parasite-free animals.

Uses of ash wood

Ash wood has been important for people for thousands of years not only as a readily available source of renewable fuel but also for making cartwheels, furniture and the handles of tools and weapons. It has also been used as a herbal medicine. An infusion of leaves can help detoxify the body by speeding up the excretion of urea and also working as a laxative; the ancient Greeks brewed tea from ash leaves to treat rheumatism. Ash has played a significant role in Britain's military history. The English longbow was made of imported yew wood, but its arrows were produced from straight prominent-grained ash: 'At the battle of Agincourt in 1415, 1,000 arrows were fired every second.'[2]

1. Deakin 2016, p. 386.
2. 'The Longbow', October/November 1999, www.history-magazine.com/longbow.html, accessed February 2016.

Calke Abbey

Derbyshire

The south front of Calke Abbey.

Calke Abbey has often been referred to as 'the house that time forgot' and this may also be applied to the trees in the extensive parkland that surrounds it. The Harpur family bought the estate in 1622 and for centuries were well known for being rather eccentric and reclusive. They were reluctant to keep up with the latest technology such as electricity, which they did not install until 1962. When the National Trust acquired the Abbey in 1985 it effectively inherited a time capsule: the house was largely unmodernised and the old trees in the woods and parklands had been allowed to age, decline and decay.

Today Calke Abbey has some of the finest ancient trees in the country and, because of the wealth of fallen and rotting timber, is among the top ten locations in Britain for beetles that live on decaying wood. With more than 550 species of invertebrates, around 350 of which are beetles such as the rare cobweb beetle (*Ctesias serra*), the grounds are now a National Nature Reserve (NNR) and a Site of Special Scientific Interest (SSSI).

One of the most remarkable of all the ancient trees is a small-leaved lime (*Tilia cordata*), which can be found close to the main car park. When head ranger Bill Cove was looking through the property archives, he discovered a reference to it in a nineteenth-century edition of the *Derby Mercury* newspaper as the largest small-leaved lime in the country, 'standing nearly 100ft tall and with a girth of 72 feet'. Today it is still huge but in its old age some of its enormous bole has tumbled down the steep bank on which it stands. It is unusual for a small-leaved lime to grow to such a size in Britain.

By far the most numerous type of ancient tree in the Abbey park is the oak (*Quercus*). Two of the finest and oldest are known as the 'Old Man of Calke' and the 'Elder Oak', which have girths in excess of 9 metres. Oaks with a circumference of this size are thought to be at least 800 years old; the 'Old Man of Calke' is estimated to be up to 1,200 years old. Both trees have been pollarded over many centuries, which has enabled them to reach such a great age.

Near to the 'Old Man of Calke' is one of the best examples in Britain of a 'walking tree' (see also Blickling, p. 27). Here, two new trees are set a short distance from the main stem of the old lime. One is connected while the other is now independent but still displaying what looks like a navel where it was formerly linked to its 'mother'. The 'walking' process may have repeated itself over thousands of years and, as each new tree is a clone of the original, so it could be argued that this group of trees is part of an organism that has continued to exist for more than 10,000 years.

The magnificent lime (*Tilia*) avenue, which lines the approach to the house.

Overleaf: An enormous ancient small-leaved lime tree (*Tilia cordata*), which was one of the largest in Britain before part of the main trunk collapsed.

The famous 'walking lime tree' (*Tilia cordata*).

Avenues of trees have been popular for centuries and the remnants of those planted in the seventeenth and early eighteenth century can still be seen. These typically comprised oak, elm (*Ulmus*) or chestnut (*Castanea*) and were designed to align with the axis of a mansion. However, by the eighteenth century it was fashionable to use hybrid lime trees (*Tilia*) and in 1846 a new avenue of 82 lime trees was planted to celebrate the birth of Vauncey Harpur-Crewe, last Baronet of Calke. They now form a dramatic entrance to the Abbey.

The Old Man of Calke is an oak (*Quercus*) with a girth of over 9 metres, which is considered to be around 1,200 years old.

Clumber Park
Nottinghamshire

Clumber Park has the longest double avenue of common lime trees (*Tilia x Europaea*) in Europe.

Clumber Park is home to many ancient trees including one of the largest beeches (*Fagus sylvatica*) in Britain. It is also famous for having the longest double lime (*Tilia*) avenue in Europe.[1]

The park was created in 1707 after John Holles, 1st Duke of Newcastle, successfully petitioned Queen Anne for 'a licence to make a Park in the forest of Sherwood in the County of Nottingham for her Majesty's services during her life time to contain at least 3000 acres [1215 hectares] of his Own lands of inheritance'.[2] The park once formed part of Sherwood Forest, renowned for its association with the outlaw and cultural hero Robin Hood. Like Clumber today the vast ancient area was not continuously forested but comprised a mosaic of wooded areas, grassland, patches of scrub, thorns and brambles, old pollard trees and agricultural settlements.

The Bundle Beech (*Fagus sylvatica*) is one of the largest in Britain and spectacular in autumn.

The various Dukes of Newcastle went on to shape the parkland over the next 200 years until it was acquired by the National Trust in 1945. The purchase by the Trust saved hundreds if not thousands of ancient and veteran trees because by 1937 Clumber Park had fallen into serious financial difficulties and parcels of land were already being sold off. When the estate at Clumber was put up for sale in the 1940s local timber merchants were keen to purchase the land and cut down the remaining trees for timber.[3]

The Bundle Beech

The 'Bundle Beech' (*Fagus sylvatica*) is among the largest trunked and most spectacular trees at Clumber with a huge girth of nearly 8 metres. One of the explanations for its name is that, on closer inspection, the vast fluted trunk looks as though it might be eight distinct trees that have grown and fused together. It was thought at first that this was the result of eight tree seedlings being planted in close proximity although now it is believed that it could simply be a case of the tree dividing into separate functional units.

Trees are radically different from animals in their strategies to protect themselves. One of their main problems is that they cannot move, which makes them vulnerable to damage caused by insects, fungi, large animals and man, as well as fires and storms. In response they have evolved to become incredible survivors, spreading their risk by being able to divide into units that function fairly independently.

The lime avenue

From the seventeenth century onwards it was fashionable on country house estates to plant formal avenues as a statement of wealth. These were bold and highly visible structures that took considerable resources to create and maintain. By the nineteenth century the vogue was to use exotic hybrid trees in place of native species. In Holland new hybrids of lime trees had been developed around 1840 and Henry Pelham-Clinton, 4th Duke of Newcastle, arranged for a double avenue of this new species of lime to be planted at Clumber Park. The avenue leads from the main north-east entrance of the estate towards the house stretching for more than 3.2 kilometres (2 miles) and has no fewer than 1,296 trees.

Lime trees are linked to justice and peace throughout Europe. They were usually planted to mark significant historical events, such as the end of the battle of Fribourg in 1644, and many of the 60,000 trees planted to commemorate the advent of the first 'Republic of France' in 1792 were limes.[4]

Forestry workers bringing timber in with heavy horses at Clumber Park, *c.*1900.

Sherwood Forest

Sherwood Forest encompassed an area that included woodland, farming and grazing land, and settlements. It is well documented and historic charters give a fascinating insight into the types of rights and activities that were current around the time the Domesday Book was completed in 1086. For example, John, the Earl of Morton (brother of King Richard I), granted to Ralph FitzStephen and his wife Maud de Caux from 1175 to 1176 until their deaths in 1202 and 1224 respectively:

> all liberties and custody of the forest of Sherwood including permission to hunt hare, fox, cat, and squirrel with dogs and hounds; all windfallen wood; the valuable inner bark or bast of the lime trees; a skep out of every cartload of salt passing through the forest, and half a skep from a half load; and after pannage (*retro-pannagium*) for pigs; all pleas of unlawed dogs; together with all goods and chattels belonging to thieves or 'latronis' taken by them within the forest.[5]

This shows clearly that far from being like the untamed mythical wildwood, Sherwood Forest was a hub of economic activity during the twelfth and thirteenth centuries.

1. Morrison 2002, pp. 103–18.
2. Boulton (ed.) 1965.
3. Rotherham 2007, p. 7.
4. Pigott 2005, p. 18.
5. www.robinhoodlegend.com/history-sherwood/, accessed February 2016.

Coniston
Cumbria

A working woodland

The woods that clothe the hills around Coniston Water in the Lake District are stunningly beautiful. In many respects they look like the epitome of the great wildwood, which was once thought to cover the whole of Europe. Glossy-leaved trees standing shoulder to shoulder, thickly clad with epiphytes and resounding with the calls of many different types of birds, give the woods every appearance of being natural. However, apart from the most remote gorges and stream sides, they have been heavily utilised for hundreds of years, which was something that continued until only a few generations ago.

People in the Coniston area relied on harvested wood for pit props for the mines, to make the charcoal for smelting iron and for use in the local tanning industry. Until the late nineteenth century the forests would have been alive with workers using saws and axes and generally making use of the natural products that grow there, such as mushrooms, berries and bracken for animal bedding. It is easy to forget in these modern times that these were 'working woods', managed and altered over hundreds, possibly thousands, of years but in a way that did not destroy them and which in many cases supported the trees to live to greater ages while at the same time enhancing local biodiversity.

The largest alder (*Alnus glutinosa*) in Britain, which is close to the north end of Coniston Water, shed an enormous branch in 2014.

The great alder

Just a short distance north of the tip of Coniston Water grows Britain's largest alder (*Alnus glutinosa*), which has a girth of 6.47 metres. The old tree has reached a point where it is declining and in 2014 one of the huge lateral branches fell to the ground. The fallen timber will now begin the process of rotting down and providing additional microhabitats, which will in turn be able to support even more species of wildlife.

Along with willow (*Salix*), alder is Britain's most common riverside tree; both thrive in heavily waterlogged soil. Sometimes referred to as the 'water king', alder grows well in boggy land or along the edges of rivers and is the only native British tree whose seeds can be dispersed using water: each seed

An ancient small-leaved lime (*Tilia cordata*), which is more than 1,500 years old, on the steep slopes around Coniston.

has a tiny air bag to help floatation. The timber is particularly durable underwater and it is for this reason that it has been traditionally used in pilings, jetty poles, sluices and waterside buildings; indeed much of Venice is supported by alder pilings. Alder was once actively planted along watercourses near areas of industry because it was considered the best material for making clogs during the Industrial Revolution.

Lime ancients

In contrast to most of the Coniston woodland and hidden in the ghylls (steep-sided valleys with fast flowing streams) are ancient lime woodlands which, because of their inaccessibility, particularly to sheep, have remained virtually unchanged since the last Ice Age, 12,000 years ago. Within these tiny remnants of woodland are giant small-leaved lime trees (*Tilia cordata)* some of which are estimated to be over 1,600 years old. Even more remarkably, a number have been slowly 'walking' downhill over centuries by being washed downstream in flash floods and re-rooting wherever they came to rest.

Climate changes since the last Ice Age have resulted in small-leaved lime trees being unable to regenerate from seed in northern Britain for the last 4,400 years. It therefore could be argued that some of these ancient trees' lives started more than 5,000 years ago. Evidence gained from studying pollen recovered from the deep sediments of Coniston Water has confirmed that small-leaved lime spread into the area approximately 5,500 years ago but stopped successfully reproducing using flowers and seeds around 1,000 years later.

Even so, sprays of sweetly scented, lemon-coloured flowers destined never to set viable seed continue to be a rich source of nectar for insects such as bees and hoverflies.

Limes, love and dragons

Medieval poets regularly used lime trees as the symbol of romantic love and often described lovers lying on 'sweet-smelling flowers', which caused them to become intoxicated: they are thought to have been referring partly to lime blossom.

In the famous *A Modern Herbal*, written by Mrs Grieve in 1931, a note of caution was added about using a centuries-old medicinal remedy of lime-flower tea. It was said that the tea, when made with flowers that were too old, could induce 'symptoms of narcotic intoxication'.[1]

In ancient European mythology limes were represented as female and were associated with the goddess of love and fertility, Freya, along with the goddess of married love and the hearth, Frigga, by the early Norse and Germanic peoples.

1. Grieve 1931, p. 486.

The small-leaved lime (*Tilia cordata*) woodland in the inaccessible gullies around Coniston is considered to be virtually unchanged since the retreat of the ice sheets 12,000 years ago.

Croft Castle
Hertfordshire

Wood warbler (*Phylloscopus sibilatrix*).

It was in July 1588, following the first skirmish with the Spanish Armada off the south coast of Britain, that Sir Francis Drake disobeyed orders and slipped away from his fleet to loot two incapacitated Spanish galleons. He was in search of gold and gunpowder but among the provisions he probably would have found barrels of sweet chestnuts as these were one of the staple foods in the Mediterranean region at the time.

Croft Castle is home to several hundred ancient sweet chestnut trees (*Catanea sativa*), also known as Spanish chestnuts. They are all believed to be over 400 years old and are reputed to have been grown from seeds salvaged from a sinking Spanish galleon of the Armada. While this is not certain, the size and appearance of the trees growing today does correspond closely to other trees of around the same age. Furthermore, it is known that dozens of the fleeing Spanish galleons were pushed onto rocks in the Irish Sea during a ferocious storm, no doubt scattering the coastline with debris. It would seem that somehow a barrel of these nutritious seeds made its way to Croft where they are believed to have been planted in celebration of the British victory. In the sixteenth century the British were not used to eating chestnuts and would have been more likely to plant them than eat them: a fact that made the British writer John Evelyn despair, particularly when he witnessed the proteinaceous seeds being fed to pigs. He famously described the nuts as a 'food for princes and a lusty and masculine food for rusticks, and able to make women well complexioned.'[1]

Today at Croft there is an avenue of sweet chestnut trees, huge and imposing, which stretches away from the main building in a line for over 500 metres. It is said that in this part of the estate the ranks of gnarled and twisted old chestnuts are supposed to replicate one of the Armada's battle formations. While the trees remain resplendent in their rugged glory, sadly the avenue has been struck by *Phytophthora cinnamomi*, a disease that is working its way along the interconnected roots and gradually killing these magnificent specimens. There are great snagged branches in their reduced canopies and the ground around their enormous trunks is now strewn with woody limbs, some of which look as though they are twisted in pain. Through the eyes of the cinema-goer it could be the aftermath of a battle involving 'ents' (tree people) from J.R.R. Tolkien's *Lord of the Rings* (1954). While the trees are very obviously in decline, the rotten heartwood and fallen branches are providing habitats for an array of fungi, saproxylic invertebrates (insects that feed on decaying wood) and their associated predators, such as flycatchers, woodpeckers, warblers and several species of rare British bats. Walking along the avenue of these contorted and decaying ancients in the

The Quarry Oak (*Quercus petraea*) is the oldest and largest oak tree at Croft Castle and has a girth of almost 11 metres.

Knighting the Captains on board the 'Ark Royal', by Bernard Finegan Gribble (1873–1962), *c.*1935–36. The avenue of Spanish chestnuts (*Castanea sativa*) at Croft Castle is believed to have been planted from seeds salvaged from a sinking ship of the Spanish Armada.

knowledge that they are all edging towards inevitable collapse and death is a somewhat sobering experience. Yet at the same time it is a privilege to be able to stand among these time-worn trees, which have such a fascinating historical resonance.

It was Frances Kilvert in 1876 who famously described the ancient trees of nearby Moccas Park as 'those grey, gnarled, low browed, knock kneed, bent, huge, strange, long armed, deformed, hunchbacked, misshapen oak men that stand awaiting and watching century after century.'[2] However, today this may be a more apt description for the ageing ranks of Spanish chestnuts at Croft Castle.

While the chestnuts at Croft may be ancient in a British context, they are still young when compared to the largest and oldest specimen in the world, found in Sicily in 1770, which was measured as having a girth of 62 metres.

The Quarry Oak

The ancient Spanish chestnuts may be numerous at Croft but are by no means the oldest specimens. The park is also full of great ancient oaks (*Quercus*) many of which have girths in excess of 7 metres; the largest, known as the 'Quarry Oak', has a girth of almost 11 metres. An oak of this size is generally regarded as being around 1,000 years old. As its name suggests,

Part of the long avenue of ancient Spanish chestnuts (*Castanea sativa*).

The unusual orchard of hawthorn pollards (*Crataegus monogyna*) at the western end of the grounds.

it is located in a former quarry where stone was excavated for the construction of the castle. It is a magnificent tree and has a wonderfully colourful and curiously dimpled trunk, covered in lichens and moss.

Ancient hawthorns

It is important to note that the term 'ancient' is particular for each type of tree. For oak and yew 'ancient' may mean over 600 years old, but for other species such as birch and rowan it could be as little as 150 years. At the very far end of the chestnut avenue at Croft is an area of ancient hawthorn trees (*Crataegus monogyna*). The trees form an orchard and could each be more than 200 years old, which is a truly significant age for hawthorn. Standing only 4 metres tall, they display evidence of having been regularly pollarded throughout their lives. But why would you have an orchard of hawthorn trees? And why pollard them over such a long period of time? Indeed, while edible, the fruit of the hawthorn is not appealing for human consumption. However, their dense prickly branches have been employed for centuries to plug holes in hedges to deter animals. It is thought that they may also have been used at Croft as the root stock for grafting on fruit trees, much in the same way that apple varieties are grafted onto crab apple stems. Medlar (*Mespilus germanica*), a fruit much loved up until the mid-nineteenth century, was often grafted onto hawthorn root stock. Whatever the reason, because of the pollarding, the hawthorn trees have lived far longer than they would normally without intervention.

1. Evelyn 1725
2. Quoted in Lockwood 1990, p. 134.

Overleaf: Pollard oak (*Quercus*) at Croft Castle.

Crom Estate
County Fermanagh

Situated on the edge of Lough Erne near Enniskillen in Northern Ireland, and next to the crumbling ruins of the original Crom Castle, stand two of Britain's most wonderful yew trees (*Taxus baccata*). Generally yews are considered to be sombre and somewhat sepulchral because of their associations with graveyards and death. However, at Crom Castle, what looks like one giant spreading yew tree was once renowned as a place of fun and festivities.

In the nineteenth century Crom Castle was famous for claiming to have 'the largest yew in the British Isles'. However it transpired on closer inspection that, rather than the vast tangle of layering branches being just a single individual, it was actually a conjoined pair of umbriferous male and female English yews. Today they still have an impressive combined circumference of 35 metres and a diameter of 10.6 metres, but an enormous specimen at Shugborough in Shropshire now has the record for the largest canopied yew tree in Britain.

The earliest known reference to the Crom yew was by Dr William Henry, Dean of Killaloe, who in 1739 wrote: 'In the centre of the garden stands a curious yew tree, planted about 70 years ago. Its straight stem ascends about 12 feet, thence shooting out its branches horizontally it forms a circular shade 75 feet in circumference ... impenetrable by the heaviest rain'.[1] Despite his claims that the tree was 'planted about 70 years ago', it may be that the pair are actually much older than the 300 years his estimates would have made them. In fact, recent studies by experts from the Ancient Yew Group indicate that they are more likely to be over 600 years old.

The Old Castle ruins at Crom.

Ever since Dr Henry's first description, the trees have been regularly documented. For example, in an 1835 copy of the Ordnance Survey Memoirs there is mention of how the 'Great Yew of Crom', a 'curious yew tree', was 'trained horizontally six feet six inches from the ground by beams cut from rough timber'.[2] The earliest known pictorial representation of the female tree is from an 1850 watercolour by Henry Brocas Jnr, which depicts the Viceroy, Lord Clarendon, visiting Crom amid the celebrations around the Old Castle. The picture clearly shows the tree's branches being supported by what appears to be a solid wooden frame flanked by the early Victorian parterre.

Shan Bullock, writing of his youth at Crom in the 1870s, also remembered the yew with its

> great stem rising from a heaped mound [spreading] in a circle 90 feet in diameter [and needing for] the support of its branches two circles of oak pillars carrying heavy beams...how often have I climbed that tree, turned wild cat on its beams, gathered its pink berries and sucked the sweet jelly from their bitter cores.[3]

These wooden supports, which held up the great skirts of layering branches, were still very much in evidence in 1908 when Peter Brock wrote of the female tree:

The canopy of the Crom yews (*Taxus baccata*) held up by posts, *c.*1900.

> [it] form[s] a mound 20 feet in diameter and 4 feet high and [it] has a girth of 12 feet 6 inches at one foot from the ground. The height of the tree is 22 feet 6 inches and diameter of spread of branches north to south 82 feet; east to west 71 feet ... The strongest branches extend directly outward from the pleated part and rest on a trellising of poles supported by 76 oak posts averaging 5.5 feet in height. Viewed from the eastern side, it presents the appearance of an enormous green mushroom.[4]

It was reported that at its 'formal peak' 200 people often dined under the spreading branches of the Crom yews, which were considered to be the prime attraction for nineteenth-century tourists. The trees are still remarkable and continue to draw many visitors every year. The only difference is that the framework of supporting poles that once held the canopy up over the partygoers has long since gone and the branches are now left to twist and writhe all the way to the ground. It is still possible, however, to enter into the cave-like interior and experience a reflective moment accompanied by the susurration of the wind in the feathery branches.

1. See King (ed.) 1892.
2. Day and McWilliams (eds) 1990, p. 91.
3. Bullock 1929, p. 195.
4. Brock 1908, pp. 186–87.

One of the ancient yews (*Taxus*) at Crom.

Croome Park

Worcestershire

Lancelot 'Capability' Brown (1716–83), after Sir Nathaniel Dance-Holland RA (1735–1811), *c.*1770–75.

Home to many elegant and ancient trees, Croome Park illustrates the extraordinary dichotomy that is a feature of many of the National Trust's properties. Croome is treasured for its designed vistas, manicured gardens, classic buildings and exotic tree plantings while at the same time the more rustic outlying areas are also recognised for their remarkable trees and woodlands, which provide valuable wildlife habitats and a link to an earlier landscape.

One of the grand cedars of Lebanon (*Cedrus libani*) planted by Capability Brown around the rotunda.

Comprising a large house, gothic church and a series of wonderful follies, the landscape is highly man-made. Lancelot 'Capability' Brown was hired in 1751 by the 6th Earl of Coventry, who had just inherited Croome and aspired to the latest in tasteful and stylishly designed estates. It was to be Brown's first major commission, marking a key moment in English landscape design that would go on to be replicated numerous times across Britain.

Croome takes its name from the small river (O/E *croome* meaning 'small winding stream') that snakes across a shallow valley of rather unproductive wetlands. Brown, who started his work in 1752, was bold; he drained the wetlands with miles of pipes and moved the village out of view of the park before designing a landscape on a grand scale.

The planting of trees and shrubs was important to Brown as they helped contribute to the design and could be used to create some of the illusions he desired. However, in the construction of what some people felt was a 'masterpiece of landscape design', he may also have removed many important native trees. The boggy valley would have been an ideal location for willow (*Salix*) and stream-side alders (*Alnus*) and possibly the haunt of the now rare bittern. In later projects he incorporated some of the most impressive trees into his grand designs. What was exceptional about Brown was his vision. He seemed able to visualise a landscape complete with mature trees, which would exist only well after his lifetime. Many of the trees planted by Brown still survive at Croome today, including planes (*Platanus*), cedars (*Cedrus*) and cypresses (*Chamaecyparis* and *Cupressus*). By the early

Many different types of trees were planted as part of the landscaping by Brown, including London plane trees (*Platanus x acerifolia*).

nineteenth century Croome became well known for its vast tree and plant collections and was described as 'second only to Kew' for its botanical diversity.[1]

The trees that grow around the restored Grade I-listed rotunda (built between 1754 and 1757), a domed circular building close to the main house, are a masterpiece in their own right. Elegant, feathery-branched cedars of Lebanon (*Cedrus libani*), now more than 200 years old, partly enclose the building but a gap within the trees leads to an expansive view down to the main house and landscaped valley. Brown often used exotic tree species in his designs, and cedars in particular, not only for their beautiful shape, but also for their deep cultural significance with which he created classic timeless landscapes. The insight that allowed Brown to conceive of the sheer delight that his tree planting would engender hundreds of years after his death, when many of the trees would be reaching their prime, was extraordinary.

An ancient oak tree (*Quercus*) standing in a part of Croome Park that remains a more agricultural 'undesigned' landscape.

To the north of the rotunda in a more agricultural 'undesigned' landscape stands the oldest tree on the estate. This solitary oak (*Quercus*), with its gnarled and bulbous trunk, has been growing here for over 600 years. Like many ancient oaks it has been pollarded. Significantly, the older the oak, the more valuable it is in promoting wildlife; rare invertebrates are attracted to the crumbling heartwood as the core of the tree gradually rots. The dead wood in the canopy is colonised by a host of different invertebrate species, which in turn attract predatory insects and birds, such as greater spotted woodpeckers (*Dendrocopos major*) and tree creepers (*Certhia familiaris*), as well as beetle-eating noctule (*Nyctalus noctula*) and serotine (*Eptesicus serotinus*) bats.

Lord Coventry, who had seen Capability Brown only a few days before his death in 1783, acknowledged his achievements at Croome with an inscription on a monument near the lake that reads:

> 'TO THE MEMORY OF LAUNCELOT BROWN,
> WHO, BY THE POWERS OF HIS INIMITABLE AND
> CREATIVE GENIUS, FORMED THIS GARDEN
> SCENE OUT OF A MORASS.'

1. Young 2012, p. 465.

Dinefwr

Carmarthenshire

Situated on the edge of Llandeilo, Dinefwr is the most significant ancient tree site in Wales, recognised by its National Nature Reserve (NNR) status; it is the only parkland NNR in Wales. This very special landscape is full of history and lore. Dinefwr Castle, now a ruin in the ownership of Cadw, the Welsh government's historic environment service, was built in the twelfth century and was fought over, destroyed, dismantled and rebuilt several times until 1660, when Newton House was built and the Castle kept as a summer house. For years it was the seat of the king of much of Wales.

White cattle

Throughout the turbulent period of the Castle's history, and indeed well before it was built, Dinefwr white cattle grazed the park. When Hywel Dda, the early tenth-century king, codified the laws of Wales (Yfraith Hywel or Laws of Hywel, also known as Welsh Law), these cattle were used as a form of currency: tithes and fines had to be paid with the animals.

White cattle herd at Dinefwr.

Dinefwr is their ancestral home. Sadly, the white herd were sold in the 1970s when the estate was broken up, but the National Trust reintroduced them in 1992 from the same blood lines.

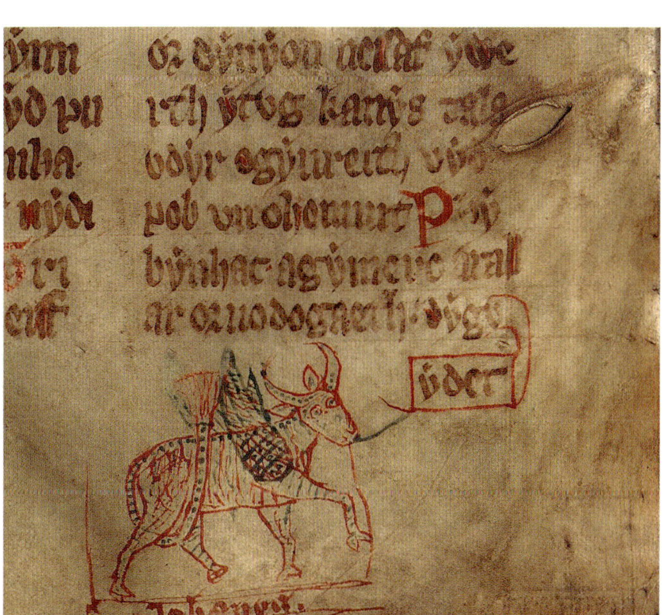

A Welsh text of the Laws of Hywel Dda, copied *c.*1350.

The deer park

Walking through the gate into the deer park is like stepping back into medieval Wales, where white cattle and fallow deer (*Dama dama*) graze among ancient sessile oaks (*Quercus petraea*) and pedunculate oaks (*Quercus robur*). In spring there are carpets of bluebells (*Hyacinthoides*), as well as dead wood in the trees and on the ground, slowly decaying and recycling the nutrients. If you replaced the white cattle with aurochs, it could be a scene straight from the wildwood of prehistory, once assumed to be an impenetrable dark dank forest, but now believed to have been a mosaic of trees, grassland and scrub, just like the deer park. This is a land of ancient trees:

The huge trunk of an ancient ash tree (*Fraxinus excelsior*).

in excess of 300 trees over 400 years old have so far been recorded and there are many more to find. It is therefore not surprising to learn that Dinefwr may be the oldest continually active deer park in Wales.

You could be excused for thinking that, with so many dead trees lying about and living trees with exposed decaying trunks, this must be an unhealthy forest, possibly suffering from some disease. Nothing could be further from the truth. Here we are given an insight into how a natural unmanaged 'wildwood' should look. There is a strict policy of not removing any of the fallen or dead trees from the deer park, so rare in our overly tidy world. This practice is what makes Dinefwr such a special place, not just aesthetically but also for the wildlife associated with decaying trees. The trees provide the material, but the fungi do the essential work of breaking down the unpalatable wood to allow specialist saproxylic invertebrates to digest it; these, in turn, are food for birds and bats.

On a bank beside the boardwalk running through the wetland known as the Bog Wood, there is one particularly

Dinefwr Castle from South West, Welsh School, *c.*1710–30.

impressive oak (*Quercus*), the 'Castle Oak'. Estimated to be about 700 years old, it stands out with its girth of 8.68 metres, making it the biggest and probably the oldest living thing at Dinefwr.

Ash trees

While the oak may be the oldest, an even more exceptional tree is situated in the park to the north of the driveway to Newton House, standing on its own. At first glance it looks unimpressive, but once you are close to it you realise this is a very ancient ash (*Fraxinus excelsior*). With a girth of 6.24 metres it would be 450 years old, but much of the tree has decayed and it has fragmented into two individuals, so its historic girth might have been much larger.

Until recently, within the deer park there was another wonderful ancient ash, possibly even older: a massive hollow tree with a mature 150-year-old oak growing out of its decayed centre. Sadly, the ash died, collapsed and left little evidence of this once great tree.

Interestingly, *Fraxinus* species often exude a sugary substance, which the ancient Greeks called *méli*, that is, honey. This was harvested commercially until the early part of the twentieth century, and is found in *Fraxinus excelsior* in northern Europe and *Fraxinus ornus* in the mountains of Greece. It is this feature that is believed to have given rise to the idea of a golden age when 'men ate acorns and honey that dripped from trees'. Ash tree nymphs were said to have nursed the infant Zeus by feeding him honey.

Fallow deer in the deer park at Dinefwr.

Dunham Massey

Cheshire

Dunham Massey has been a deer park for more than 700 years and has herds of fallow deer (*Dama dama*) roaming the grounds.

Dunham Massey, originally known as 'Old Park', is located close to the town of Altrincham. Acquired by the National Trust in 1976 it covers approximately 120 hectares and is famous for its deer park. What is special about the park is that it is one of the few in Britain that have been continuously maintained as a deer park, from the time that it was first mentioned in 1353.[1] Although deer parks date back to the Anglo-Saxons, most were created between 1100 and 1350, after the arrival of the Normans. In their heyday in 1300, the historian Oliver Rackham estimates that there would have been around 3,200 parks in England.[2] Because of the cost of the upkeep of the high fences and deep ditches most had fallen into disuse by the end of the English Civil War in 1651.

The parks were much more than just about deer; they were multi-functional enterprises providing the local economy with a variety of resources besides venison. These included firewood and timber, land for agriculture, and grazing for cattle and horses, as well as opportunities for mining.

By 1792 timber sales accounted for 20 per cent of the Dunham estate's income. Today the park has one of the densest concentrations of ancient and veteran trees in the north-west of England. Sturdy oaks (*Quercus*) and large sweet chestnuts (*Castanea sativa*) proliferate, while graceful lime (*Tilia*) avenues line much of the extensive network of paths. Among the beeches (*Fagus*) is a particularly magnificent tree located towards the eastern extent of the park close to the A55 road. In response to a root fungus known as giant polypore (*Meripilus giganteus*), its great grey rippling root plate spreads out like molten wax from the base of a candle. As the tree's roots were decayed by the fungus, the tree responded by stimulating extensive reactive growth, creating its root plate as well as growing new healthy roots to keep it stable against high winds and to maintain the supply of nutrients and water to its leaves.

In response to a fungus (*Meripilus giganteus*), this large beech's (*Fagus sylvatica*) roots have spread out like wax from a candle base.

Dead wood, beetles and the magnificent seven

From the middle of the nineteenth century, scientists and beetle enthusiasts have recognised the importance of the insects attracted to the dead wood of Dunham's ancient trees: 227 species of dead-wood beetles have been recorded, 65 of which are said to be nationally scarce. In 2008 seven species of

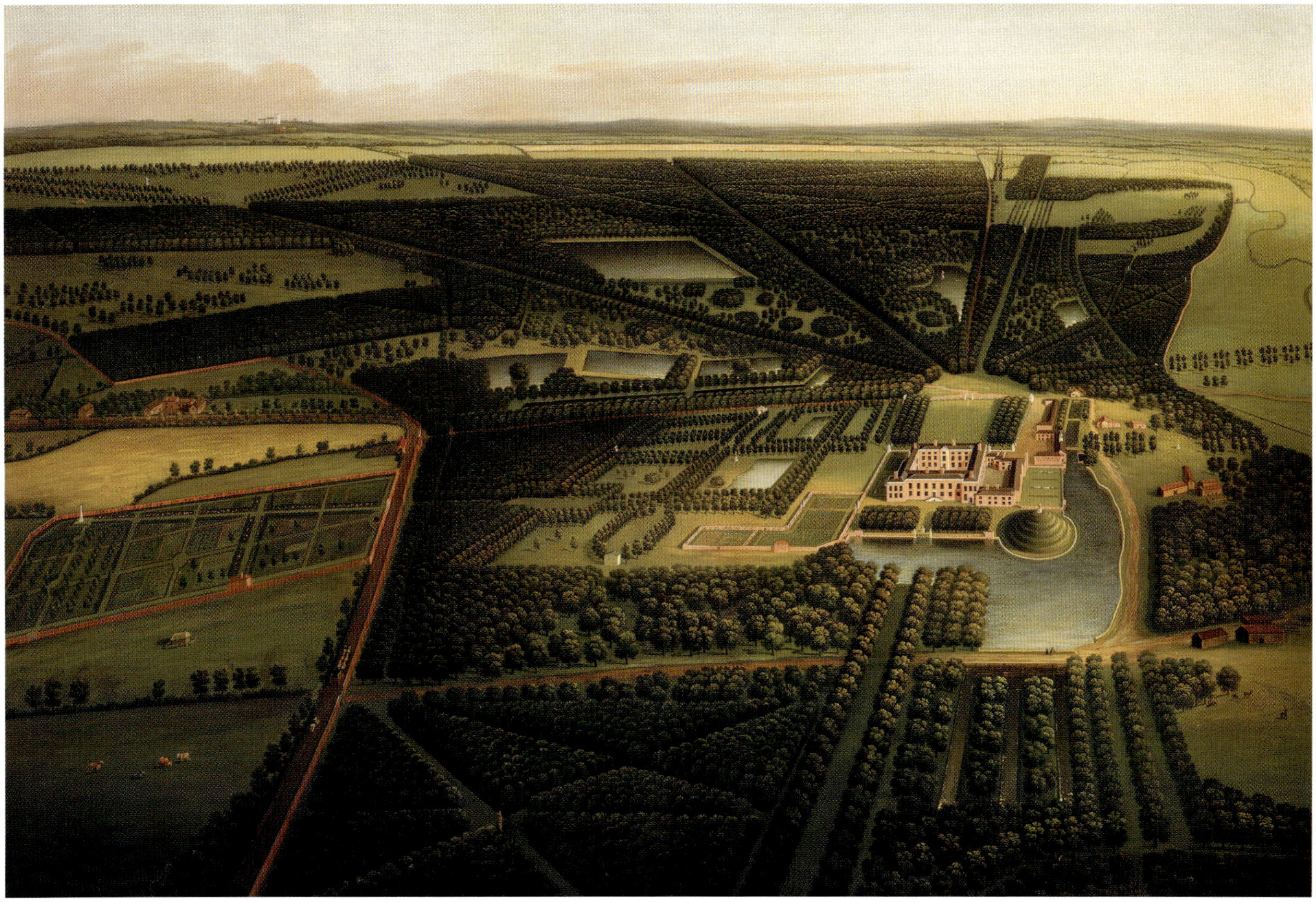

A Bird's Eye View of Dunham Massey from the North, by John Harris (1715–55), *c.*1750.

beetle were rediscovered in the park after last being seen there over 100 years ago. These included the rare flat bark beetle (*Pediacus depressus*) and the nationally rare false darkling beetle (*Abdera quadrifasciata*), which thrives in dead aerial branches of open-grown broadleaved trees. Other remarkable finds were the darkling beetle (*Pseudocistela ceramboides*) and the hister beetle (*Aeletes atomarius*).

At Dunham Massey, yellow meadow ants (*Lasius flavus*) flourish in the meadows where deer graze rather than horses or cattle, both of which damage the ant hills. There is also the fungus gnat (*Scythropochroa quercicola*), which can survive only on a fungus that lives on dead wood; the insect is known at just two other sites in Britain.

A view of the grand house across the lake.

1. Baines 1868.
2. Rackham 1980, p. 191.

The large collection of open-grown old oaks (*Quercus*) at Dunham Massey is typical of a deer park.

Female darkling beetle (*Pseudocistela sp.*).

An ancient oak (*Quercus*) showing signs of fire damage, which in this case was caused by an incendiary bomb during the Second World War.

Emmetts Garden
Kent

One of several spectacular handkerchief trees (*Davidia involucrata*) brought back to Emmetts by Wilson.

Every May in the exquisitely manicured 1.6-hectare garden at Emmetts, near Sevenoaks, there is a striking display by a particular tree whose large blousy flowers flutter like white handkerchiefs. Known as the 'handkerchief' or 'dove' tree (*Davidia involucrata*), it is one of a group grown from seed collected by the Victorian botanist Ernest Wilson on his first expedition into the wilds of Asia in 1899 in search of exotic plants. These beautiful trees are a little over 100 years old, which means they are the most ancient of their species to be found in Europe. It is not just their age that is interesting but also the extraordinary story of their discovery and transportation to Britain.

Handkerchief trees are native to China and were once regarded as the 'holy grail' of Victorian plant collectors. It is hard to imagine the excitement that these trees, now readily available in garden centres across Britain, generated back in the late 1890s. It was at that time that stories of the discoveries of the legendary French priest and naturalist Father Armand David came to the attention of Britain's most eminent horticulturalist, Sir Harry Veitch, the founder of the Chelsea Flower Show.

It was Augustine Henry's description in 1888 of a tree that 'seemed as though the branches had been draped in thousands of ghostly-white handkerchiefs', which caught Veitch's imagination.[1] He commissioned Ernest Wilson to travel to China with instructions to locate the tree and bring back viable seeds.

Wilson had shown great promise as a botanist but, even so, he was just 22 years old when he began his extraordinary journey. With typical Victorian stoicism and determination he set sail, first to the Arnold Arboretum in the United States of America to learn about the latest techniques of preserving and transporting plant specimens, and then on to China. There he met with Henry in Szemao, the only Westerner who knew the exact location of a handkerchief tree. Despite having seen it around 11 years earlier Henry was still able to pinpoint its position on a map.

Wilson's journey to a remote area of the Yunnan region was eventful: he survived serious illness, attacks by bandits and almost drowned when the boat in which he was travelling overturned. When he finally arrived at the spot Henry had marked on the map the tree had recently been felled for firewood! Undeterred, Wilson remembered that Father David had noted similar trees in Yichang, in Hubei province. It took Wilson a further two years before he could find another specimen.

When Wilson returned to England in April 1902, in addition to his prized handkerchief tree, he had amassed viable seeds of a further 304 species. Wilson is famous for being one of the greatest plant collectors of his time and the handkerchief trees in Emmetts Garden stand as a monument to his work.

1. O'Brien 2011, p. 79.

The great plant collector Ernest Wilson (centre with beard) with Sherpas on a houseboat in China.

Felbrigg and Sheringham

Norfolk

Felbrigg and Sheringham are under the same management, and both have a superb collection of mature and ancient native and exotic trees.

Felbrigg

The name Felbrigg alludes to the invasions by the Danes in the first millennium. 'Fiolbrygga' is ancient Scandinavian for a plank bridge and was first referred to in the Domesday book as *Felebruge*. Within the grounds that surround the seventeenth-century Felbrigg Hall near Cromer, 261 ancient and veteran trees have been recorded. The parkland and deer park close to the house are particularly rich in large open-grown trees, predominantly elegant ash (*Fraxinus excelsior*), gnarled sweet chestnuts (*Castanea sativa*) and stately oaks (*Quercus*).

A male redstart (*Phoenicurus phoenicurus*).

Even in the main car park it is possible to witness a wonderful ancient sweet chestnut with its huge spiralling trunk. Many sweet chestnuts have a corkscrew twist to their trunks, which becomes more pronounced as they age. The twisted grain makes them worthless for woodworkers as the cut timber has no strength. This might explain why there are such a large number of ancient sweet chestnuts across Britain. Over the centuries, in the grounds of country houses, they have been kept for aesthetic reasons, rather than for their timber.

The Great Wood

North from the main house and including what was the historic deer park is the Great Wood, dominated in part by towering beech trees (*Fagus sylvatica*) of great height and beauty. Although the beech wood appears to be a recent plantation, it was actually created over 300 years ago by the Windham family, when it comprised beech trees with an understorey of sweet chestnut coppice.

Today, epiphytic plants such as lichens and mosses abound on the fallen dead wood and in the hollows of the tree trunks. These provide an important habitat for insects, which in turn are food for birds and mammals. The site has been listed as an SSSI for its lichen species (such as *Graphis elegans* and *Parmelia purlata*) that are more commonly found in western and southern Britain, insects including two rare flies (*Triphleba excisa* and *Mycetophila lubomirski*) and woodland birds like the redstart (*Phoenicurus phoenicurus*) and the wood warbler (*Phylloscopus sibilatrix*). Recent studies of the beech

The great 1507 sessile oak (*Quercus petraea*) growing near the main house at Felbrigg, which has a hollow large enough for ten people to stand up inside.

wood revealed 33 new species of insects not previously found in Norfolk, nine of which are listed in the *Red Data Book* and include the slender or lemon slug (*Malacolimax tenellus*).

As with many beech woods the soft-barked trees have attracted graffiti artists. On several large specimens there are a series of carvings where someone has vented their feelings by writing the lyrics of love songs in the bark. This is a modern manifestation of an historic activity whereby lovers would leave secret messages on trees proclaiming their undying love for one another.

The 1507 oak

Perhaps the finest of all the trees at Felbrigg is an enormous sessile oak (*Quercus petraea*), known as the '1507 oak', which marks the boundary between Felbrigg and Aylmerton parishes. Located only a couple of minutes' walk from the main house it has a huge trunk of 9 metres in girth and great spreading branches. It is thought to originate from 1507, during the reign of King Henry VII, when landowners were under a patriotic obligation to plant oaks to help provide timber for the newly created Royal Navy. Its vast hollow is large enough to house ten people.

A View of the South Front of Sheringham Park, by Humphry Repton (1752–1818).

Love poetry carved into the soft bark of an ancient beech tree (*Fagus sylvatica*) at Felbrigg.

Sheringham

Sheringham Park covers 113 hectares and is located close to the seaside town of the same name. Although only a short distance away and under the same management as its sister park at Felbrigg, it is significantly different. This is mainly because Sheringham was created by the great landscape designer Sir Humphry Repton. He described Sheringham Park as 'my most favourite work' and today it is probably the best preserved and most intact of the more than 400 projects he undertook during his 30-year career. Repton created a 'Red Book' for each of his design projects, with artists' impressions of how the final landscaping would look.

Repton was commissioned by Abbot Upcher in 1812 to redesign Sheringham Park. Fortunately for our ancient tree heritage, Repton was quite different in his approach from the other great landscaper, Capability Brown. Repton belonged to the 'Picturesque' movement, which preferred to retain a wilder feel to the grounds surrounding the main houses. As a consequence he was far more compassionate towards old trees and ancient woodlands than was Brown, and as a by-product there are areas on the estate that are extremely rich in terms of biodiversity. These have provided islands of continuity where rare species have thrived for hundreds of years. It is perhaps to the emergence of the Picturesque movement that we owe the survival of so many remarkable trees in Britain.

One of the largest Scots pines (*Pinus sylvestris*) in Britain can be found among the ornamental plantings at Sheringham.

Scots pine

The serpentine course of the path that leads from the main car park to the house winds up and over a low hill and through a glorious arboretum of exotic trees and shrubs including Scots pine, azaleas, rhododendron and styrax species, before revealing a grand vista of parkland, woodland and a backdrop of the North Sea beyond.

Scots pine (*Pinus sylvestris*) is north-west Europe's only native pine. It is also the world's most widely distributed conifer, ranging from Ireland to Japan. Scots pine is a misnomer as the majority are found throughout Asia. The tree is especially significant for the indigenous peoples of Siberia. The Buriats, who live close to Lake Baikal, enter sacred groves of Scots pine in the same way as people would a cathedral in Britain: in silence out of respect to the gods and spirits they believe inhabit the forest. Pines in general have a rich folklore. In Greek mythology the pine tree was a symbol of royalty and associated with the goddess Pitthea.

Scots pines can survive for more than 1,000 years, particularly at the extremes of their distribution. They are valuable trees for timber and resin. In addition the resin and needles contain chemicals with antiseptic properties and are used to make preparations for the treatment of a variety of ailments, including respiratory disorders.

Florence Court

County Fermanagh

The Irish yew is a familiar sight in churchyards and gardens around the world. It is a variety of the common yew (*Taxus baccata*), which has a distinctive vertical or columnar form.

George Willis discovered the tree while strolling on the hills close to his home in County Fermanagh, Northern Ireland, in 1767. Noticing a pair of unusual young yews, he returned later to dig them up. He presented one tree to William Cole, the owner of Florence Court (later to become the first Earl of Enniskillen), and decided to raise the other in his own nursery. But even though he provided the very best growing conditions it died. Cole was probably unaware of the extraordinary rarity of the specimen he had been given. It was planted in a boggy, rather unloved, corner of the estate at Florence Court where, against all expectations, it thrived.

This variety of yew is known as *Taxus baccata var. fastigiata*. 'Fastigiate' is descriptive of a plant whose shoots and branches tend to grow parallel to the main stem, which creates its unusual upright appearance. No other example has ever been discovered. Curiously, despite the original Irish yew being female and covered in seeds each year, no new trees have ever been grown from seed; when germinated, the seedlings revert back to the common yew variety. This is why all Irish yews across the world are either directly or indirectly descended from the single tree that continues to survive at Florence Court. It is the mother of millions of genetically identical trees. Visually it is not the most exciting specimen, but being the first and only tree of its type makes it extraordinary. Its unusual multi-stemmed nature becomes obvious when standing close to it; every branch and shoot grows vertically, seemingly reaching for the light. Yews can live for thousands of years but there is no Irish yew that can possibly be older than the one growing at Florence Court, which is now around 250 years of age.

The original Irish yew (*Taxus baccata var. fastigiata*) stands in a remote part of the grounds and no other examples have ever been found.

A fine Irish yew (*Taxus baccata var. fastigiata*), in the foreground, showing its upright form in the gardens surrounding the main house at Florence Court.

A view across the parkland to Florence Court.

Fountains and Studley Royal

North Yorkshire

Studley Royal Park and the ruins of Fountains Abbey form a single area covering 323 hectares and are located close to the town of Ripon. They are both studded with ancient trees yet are quite distinct from one another: Fountains is laid out as a garden whereas Studley Royal is a wilder deer park. In recognition of the designed landscape's international significance, Studley Royal was listed by UNESCO in 1986 as one of the few World Heritage Sites in Britain.

Fountains

On 27 December 1132, a group of 13 Cistercian monks was offered refuge by Thurstan, Archbishop of York, in the Skell valley, at a site near the present-day Ripon. The monks lived simply to begin with and on a small scale, digging a vegetable garden and creating a modest wooden oratory. It is said they survived the first winter by sleeping on straw under a large elm tree (*Ulmus*) and even eating its leaves and bark. By 1135 they had been able to attract enough people to make the settlement viable, and from then on the community began to have the resources to start the construction of the famous Fountains Abbey. Today the grounds include an historic water garden, and areas of ornamental trees and native woodland.

A view through the remaining two ancient yews (*Taxus baccata*) of the Seven Sisters towards the ruins of Fountains Abbey.

The Seven Sisters

Across Britain today there are yews (*Taxus baccata*) in churchyards that are considerable older than the church itself. The reason for this is that churches were often deliberately constructed on former religeo-pagan sites and this may well have been the case at Fountains Abbey. The first reference to the yews known as the 'Seven Sisters' was in *The Foundation History of Fountains* (*Narratio de fundatione Fontanis monasterii*), written by Hugh, a monk of Kirkstall Abbey, in the thirteenth century. The trees were said to be 'so near to each other as to form a cover almost equal to a thatched roof'. In 1822 Jacob George Strutt, the landscape painter and etcher, visited Fountains Abbey and made engravings of five of the original seven yews, which later appeared in the seminal book *Sylva Britannica; or, Portraits of Forest Trees, distinguished for their Antiquity, Magnitude, or Beauty*. Strutt wrote:

> It is such thoughts as these that invest the venerable Yew Trees, the silent witnesses of the changes of time, and the decays of nature, with so much interest, and renders their preservation so desirable. They do not, however, appear to have been treated with the reverence due to them: a low wall hides their weather beaten boles on the side where they would otherwise have been seen to best advantage, and a paltry little stable is erected almost beneath their branches, on which, worst injury of all, the marks of the despoiling axe are but too visible.[1]

One of the surviving large yews (*Taxus baccata*) known as the Seven Sisters.

Just two of the seven trees survive on the steep slope that rises from Skelldale and Fountains Abbey. When the pioneering yew researcher Allan Meredith visited the site in 1984 he found that none of the staff was aware of the trees, which were lost in deep undergrowth; the largest had a girth of 7 metres. They are now managed by the National Trust.

The cultural importance of yew trees

Petroglyphs and runic writings suggest that the veneration of yew trees is one of the oldest forms of religious activity in Europe. Yews were important to the Romans, Greeks and Egyptians. Early sarcophagi were fashioned from the red and yellow heartwood of yews as the Egyptians believed the properties of the trees would facilitate safe passage to the afterlife. In Britain the Romans planted yews to honour their dead.[2]

For the Celts yews symbolised immortality, because they remained virtually unchanged throughout many lifetimes: a single human generation is around 25 years, so a hundred generations could have witnessed the same 2,500-year-old tree. Yews were also linked to the seasons and the sun. The scarlet arils enclosing the highly poisonous seeds that cover the female trees in winter were believed to have a connection with the return of the sun in the spring. A yew wood log (Yule log) was burnt at the Winter Solstice, the day on which the midday sun is at its lowest in the winter sky, marking the start of longer hours of daylight.

Important figures in the Middle Ages, such as the Welsh poet Dafydd ap Gwilym, often had their graves marked by the planting of a yew tree. It was also fashionable during the Victorian period for people of note to be interred beneath a yew, for example, the poet William Wordsworth and his wife Mary in the Lake District.

Engravings made by Jacob George Strutt in 1822 of the healthy-looking Seven Sisters yew trees (*Taxus baccata*).

Overleaf: An enormous ancient sweet chestnut tree (*Castanea sativa*) at Studley Royal.

Studley Royal

The history of Studley Royal's landscape can be traced back over 6,000 years, from the days of prehistoric hunters, through the rise and fall of its Cistercian monastery to today's water garden. Its former medieval deer park is home to over 300 red (*Cervus elaphus*) and sika (*Cervus nippon*) deer, which graze under some of the finest examples of ancient and veteran trees in north-eastern Britain.

Studley Royal has many well-spaced large and ancient trees, which typify a British deer park. These include enormous oaks (*Quercus*), some of which have a girth of more than 8 metres and are around 600 to 800 years old. There are also aged sweet chestnut trees (*Castanea sativa*), which are readily identified by their huge twisting trunks and long pinnate leaves.

One of the last photographs of the largest wild cherry (*Prunus avium*) in Britain in its prime at Studley Royal before the crown dramatically snapped in a freak storm in 2008.

St Mary's church is beautifully framed by the elegant avenue of hybrid lime trees (*Tilia*) that bisects Studley Royal Park.

A deer stands beside the stump of the once-great wild cherry tree (*Prunus avium*) at Studley Royal, which was the largest in Britain.

Some of these have a girth in excess of 8 metres and the oldest are 500 to 600 years old. Although the structure of deer parks has remained generally constant over hundreds of years, they do also contain examples of newer features, such as avenues. While avenues became popular from the seventeenth century onwards, the magnificent lime avenue at Studley Royal, which runs for nearly a kilometre (two-thirds of a mile), is made up of hybrid lime trees that were developed in Holland in the eighteenth century. The east–west orientation of the grand avenue means that from the midway point the trees beautifully frame St Mary's church to the west and the imposing Ripon Cathedral to the east.

Studley Royal used to be the home of Britain's largest and probably oldest wild cherry tree (*Prunus avium*). Fruit trees generally have a shorter lifespan than oaks, chestnut and limes, and 150 years is considered ancient for most cherries, apples and plums. The Studley Royal cherry is believed to be over 300 years of age and in its prime had a trunk with a girth of 5.7 metres. It was a magnificent sight each spring when its great canopy was festooned with brilliant white blossom. Unfortunately, in 2008 a freak storm snapped the trunk off about 3 metres from the ground and, while the tree survived, only the lowest branches still leaf and flower.

Early tree surgery

Some of the old oaks at Studley Royal display a curious set of hollows and holes: evidence of early tree surgery. The way ancient trees have been managed and cared for has changed dramatically over the last 100 years. Through much of the twentieth century it was considered that the rotting heartwood was detrimental to their health.[3] The solution was thought to be to create holes in the trunks and cut out the rotting internal timber. Trunks were often then bricked or even concreted up. In most cases, far from being a disastrous infection, the tree may well have stimulated fungi to begin the decay process within its heartwood.[4] Fungi break down the wood structure so releasing stored nutrients that have been locked up for hundreds of years. The tree is then able to grow aerial roots and reabsorb these nutrients, so helping it to survive long into the future.

The curious hole in one of the great oaks (*Quercus*) at Studley Royal is an early form of tree surgery. It was felt that the hollow trunk should be given air and the decaying timber removed.

1. Strutt 1830.
2. Hageneder 2007, p. 152.
3. Bridgeman 1977.
4. Lonsdale 2000.

Hadrian's Wall Estate
Northumberland

The landscape though which Hadrian's Wall runs is mostly barren, unforgiving and treeless. However, a short distance from the National Trust Housesteads Fort visitor centre and close to Milecastle 37 stands a tree that is internationally famous and which has given its name to the eponymous 'Sycamore Gap'. It has appeared in countless photographs and has even been an 'extra' in several films, including *Robin Hood: Prince of Thieves* (1991). It looks magnificent against a dramatic sky or partly buried in snow. Its location and the fact that it is a single tree on its own raise interesting questions, such as 'what were the local forests like back in Roman times' and 'is sycamore actually a native British tree or an introduced exotic species?'

The lone sycamore tree (*Acer pseudoplatanus*) at Sycamore Gap near Hadrian's Wall.

Around AD 122 the Roman emperor Hadrian decreed that a 117-kilometre (72-mile) wall be built between the River Tyne on the north-east coast of England across to the Solway Firth on the west coast. The purpose of the wall, which is also sometimes called 'Picts Wall', is not entirely clear. It could have been to defend against the marauding 'barbarians' living in the Scottish Lowlands, to delineate the extent of Hadrian's empire, or to control north–south trade. The construction was a great feat of engineering and the need for local fuel wood must have been significant. The Romans put heavy demands on timber resources wherever they went, requiring huge quantities for iron smelting, ceramics and heating (central heating in many cases) their homes. While much of the wall has fallen into disrepair, long sections still run across the undulating northern hills.

Sycamores – native or naturalised?

The sycamore (*Acer pseudoplatanus*), a type of maple, is a common sight across Britain. It can grow to 35 metres in height and live as long as 600 years. Its leaves are distinctively palmate and the bark is a pinky-grey colour, which, like the plane tree referred to in its species name (*pseudoplatanus* – false plane), develops plates when it becomes old. As sycamores mature their bark takes on a mottled appearance and the plates begin to peel off in irregular shapes exposing young healthy bark, much like our skin continually exfoliates when cells die off and are replaced.

There is considerable debate as to whether the sycamore is a native species or one that has become naturalised since

The iconic sycamore tree (*Acer pseudoplatanus*) has featured in a number of major films.

its introduction in the late fifteenth century. Many foresters regard it as a weed as it seeds extraordinarily well with its samara (winged seeds) and is therefore able to helicopter over great distances on the wind. However, Ted Green, the noted ancient tree expert and Founder President of the Ancient Tree Forum, has postulated that sycamores are indeed native to Britain and that a climatic change caused them to disappear from lowland areas leaving a few isolated pockets in the Scottish valleys. Green believes that sycamores have been present in Britain since at least the Bronze Age and maintains that pollen found in studies of Bronze Age and Iron Age burial sites could well have been mistaken for that of the field maple, whose pollen is almost identical. He has renamed the tree as the Celtic maple.

It could be that both theories of the colonisation of Britain by sycamore are correct. Sycamores may have re-colonised in a pincer movement, expanding south from trees that had survived in northern refuges while at the same time moving north from exotic trees introduced from mainland Europe in the fifteenth century as the climate changed. Either way the tree has increased in numbers and threatens many ancient habitats, previously dominated by oak, beech or ash. Some foresters have tried to reduce the impact of this increase by removing sycamore from the woodlands. However, it may be that sycamores are more suited to future climatic conditions and will continue to thrive in ancient woodlands to the detriment of other species. Time will tell.

Hatfield Forest

Essex

The hornbeam pollards (*Carpinus betulus*) have been a part of the landscape at Hatfield Forest for thousands of years.

Hatfield Forest, located east of Bishops Stortford, is considered to be the finest and best preserved medieval hunting forest in Europe. In many ways it is one of the great achievements of the National Trust, which had the foresight to acquire it in 1928 and manage it sensitively so that now, in the twenty-first century, it is still possible to 'step back in time' and wander through a landscape that has remained virtually unchanged since medieval times.

Oliver Rackham, the foremost writer and specialist on the history of British woodland, described the forest as follows:

> Hatfield is of supreme interest in that *all* the elements of a medieval Forest survive: deer, cattle, coppiced woods, pollards, scrub, timber trees, grassland and fen, plus a seventeenth-century lodge and rabbit warren. As such it is certainly unique in England and possibly the world ... The Forest owes very little to the last 250 years ... Hatfield is the only place where one can step back into the Middle Ages to see, with only a small effort of imagination, what a Forest looked like in use.[1]

An ancient field maple pollard (*Acer campestre*) in one of the wood pasture areas of Hatfield Forest.

As discussed in the introduction, many trees can attain great ages only by being managed. There are few oaks (*Quercus*) in Britain over 1,000 years old that have not been pollarded and there are no small-leaved lime trees (*Tilia cordata*) over this age that have not been coppiced repeatedly. In Rackham's opinion Hatfield Forest represents the zenith of what was possible with a wood pasture management system. Wood pasture, the maintenance of a mosaic of different areas including woodland, grassland with open-growing trees, fields and settlements, was common right across Europe from Mesolithic times. It is a practice that pre-dates deer parks and royal forests by thousands of years.

The system employed at Hatfield Forest in medieval times was extremely sophisticated. Every part of the Forest and each type of tree was managed so as to provide what was necessary to support the local population and economy, including fuel, food, fodder for grazing animals, building materials and medicinal compounds. The pollarded hornbeams (*Carpinus betulus*), for example, supplied the extremely hard and durable timber used for ox-cart axles and even the cogged mechanisms for wind and water mills. Hornbeam wood also produces a charcoal that burns at a very high temperature, making it particularly valuable for smelting metals. Today the distinctive ancient hornbeam pollards stand in the open areas with their broad squat trunks and canopies comprising many small-gauge branches. Some may be over 600 years old.

Hornbeams were just one of the economically important trees. Hatfield is believed to have been unique in Britain for the sheer variety of trees that were managed by pollarding. No fewer than eight different species have been recorded: oak,

Overleaf: Hatfield Forest is considered to be the best preserved example of a working medieval forest in the whole of Europe.

The wood from coppiced hornbeams (*Carpinus betulus*) was useful because it could be turned into a charcoal that burnt at a high enough temperature to smelt metals.

ash, maple, hornbeam, elm, beech, hawthorn and crab apple. It is unusual to find evidence of even five species of pollards in any other surviving woodland in Britain.

Timber buildings

Within a short distance of the Forest there are a number of major historic wooden buildings that were made partially or entirely from timber harvested from Hatfield. These include the Great Barn of William of Wykeham at Widdington, and Colville Hall, which is surrounded by structures that have survived from the twelfth century. Old wooden buildings can provide a snapshot of the history of ancient woodlands such as Hatfield. This is because rather than using regular rectangular beams and flat planks the carpenters of the time would have chosen local trees that naturally had the shape and properties needed for construction. The main beams in medieval buildings, for example, would often have been fashioned from a single tree, effectively preserving specimens that can now be studied. The presence of withies (thin flexible willow branches) in the wattle and daub walls provides an insight into the trees of the historic understorey too.

Around 330 trees would have been used to construct a typical fifteenth-century farmhouse in the east of England. Compared to today, the main beams were relatively small and employed timber from young oak trees that had diameters of just 25 to 30 centimetres. The length of the oak timber was important for construction. In order to create a long trunk the trees were often cultivated among a dense understorey, which prevented them from branching low down and resulted in useable sections of around 6 metres.

An ancient hornbeam pollard (*Carpinus betulus*), which has split into two separate halves.

The Doodle Oak

In Hatfield Forest, the largest oak in volume and height is the magnificent specimen that grows just north of Shell House. The trunk rises smoothly before forking into eight enormous branches, evidence that this tree once grew in tall underwood, which prevented it from sprouting branches lower down, but which has subsequently been cleared. It is estimated that today the tree represents around 22.5 cubic metres of timber and is over 300 years old.[1]

There was once an oak in the forest known as the 'Doodle Oak'. It was so spectacular that it continues to have a ghostly presence more than 150 years after its demise. The remains of its trunk can be located in an area of grassland just south of Doodle Oak Coppice. It is not clear how it attained its name but the most plausible reason it that its swollen trunk resembled the sack of a set of bagpipes, which was known by the colloquial name of a 'doodle bag'. It was already a well-known and significant tree by the seventeenth century.[3] In 1838 John Claudius Loudon measured it as '42 ft [12.8 metres] in circumference at the base; in 1813, before a large portion of the trunk fell in, it was upwards of 60 ft [16.2 metres]'.[4] At the time it was second in size only to the great 'Damory Oak' in Dorset and considerably larger than any oak alive in Britain today. There is an 1807 engraving of the tree in all its majesty, with its bulbous trunk topped by a healthy spreading crown. The engraving also clearly shows a style of pollarding known as a 'giraffe-pollard', where the tree is trimmed at a higher level than normal.

An engraving of the Doodle Oak in 1807 when it was one of the largest oaks (*Quercus*) in Europe.[2]

The Doodle Oak was last recorded alive in 1858 and nearly 100 years later the stump was excavated by Maynard Greville, whose studies suggested that the tree would have been around 15 metres in girth and 850 years old based on growth rates calculated from the small number of tree rings recovered.[5]

1. Rackham 1976.
2. Young 1807, plate 45.
3. Rackham 1993, p. 243.
4. Loudon 1838.
5. Greville 1949, pp. 1317–18.

Hughenden

Buckinghamshire

The largest and probably the oldest horse chestnut (*Aesculus hippocastanum*) in Britain is located at Hughenden. Its girth was 7.33 metres when measured in 2014. It is estimated to be over 300 years old, pre-dating the major planting projects by Benjamin Disraeli, 1st Earl of Beaconsfield and former Prime Minister, who lived in Hughenden Manor from 1848 to 1881. Prior to 2014, little attention had been given to the tree because it was tucked away in a corner by the main entrance to the property.

Horse chestnuts are very elegant; they are often the first trees to come into leaf and the first to shed them, and can grow up to 27 metres tall. They have large distinctive palmate leaves and in spring are covered in glorious white blossoms or panicles, popularly known as 'candles'. In the autumn the leaves turn rust-coloured and conkers in their prickly casings carpet the ground. In winter they have distinctive sticky red-brown buds.

Healing properties

The horse chestnut tree is prized for its medicinal properties. The seeds are poisonous to humans but contain compounds that aid circulation and relieve congestion in the veins. When made into a tincture or an ointment, they have been used as an effective remedy for the treatment of varicose veins and haemorrhoids. A chemical present in the horse chestnut, aescin, is not only an astringent but when extracted can also be particularly soothing for sprains and bruises. In Turkey, horse chestnuts were fed to horses after battle to speed up their recovery.

At risk

Unfortunately horse chestnuts are under threat within Britain and in much of Europe due to two separate issues. The first of these is the tiny horse chestnut leaf-mining moth (*Cameraria ohridella*), which was initially observed in Macedonia in 1984 and identified in Britain in Wimbledon in 2002. It is slowly progressing across England and Wales and is expected to spread throughout the UK. The minute caterpillars feed inside the leaf, reducing the tree's ability to photosynthesise, and therefore detrimentally affecting its growth. The leaves show brown lines where the caterpillars have destroyed the tissue; in acute cases the whole tree crown turns brown and the leaves fall prematurely.

The second issue is the increase in the disease known as bleeding canker (*Pseudomonas syringae pv. aesculi*), which had started to attack horse chestnuts before the arrival of leaf-mining moths. Affected trees' trunks have lesions exuding rusty-red, yellow-brown or almost black, gummy liquid. Trees that are struck by both the moths and bleeding canker usually die within a few years.

This horse chestnut (*Aesculus hippocastanum*) at Hughenden is the largest tree of its kind in Britain and is over 300 years old.

Horse chestnut (*Aesculus hippocastanum*) leaf-mining moth (*Cameraria ohridella*).

Ickworth
Suffolk

The Tea Party Oak (*Quercus robur*) is believed to be more than 700 years of age and could be older than the deer park in which it now stands.

The Tea Party Oak

At the heart of the great Ickworth estate, near the town of Bury St Edmunds, stands the extraordinary 'Tea Party Oak' (*Quercus robur*), considered to be at least 700 years old. Its immense age means that it may have been alive when the de Ickworth family first created the deer park in 1286. It is believed the tree gained its name from the regular tea parties held under its spreading branches for the benefit of the children of the nearby village of Horringer, which were organised by the 4th Marquess and Marchioness of Bristol.

The tree is one of the few constants that link Ickworth directly to its past, standing as a silent witness to great changes that have taken place over the centuries. Curiously, contrary to popular thought, there were actually fewer trees and less woodland at Ickworth in former times than there are today. Research by the great countryside historian Oliver Rackham into historic agricultural and woodland practices, especially in Essex and Suffolk, has shown that more land was under cultivation at Ickworth 700 years ago than has been the case ever since, apart from a brief period during the Second World War.[1] Rackham's examination of the Domesday records and aerial photography by the Luftwaffe during the war reveals that the forest cover of the thirteenth century around the great abbey at Bury St Edmunds (and in many other areas across England) was broadly similar to that seen in the 1940s.[2]

As a seedling the Tea Party Oak would need to have sprouted somewhere out of the reach of deer, probably in a patch of hawthorn (*Crataegus monogyna*) and bramble (*Rubus fruticosus*). Maybe the tree became a boundary marker and for this reason was left to grow to full size, but what we do know is that its branches were regularly trimmed over hundreds of years giving it the distinctive 'pollarded' shape that we see today. By the time it had reached maturity in the seventeenth century it had yet to survive 15 years of freezing winters,

Ruins in Ickworth Park, by George Quinton (*c.* 1778–1835), 1804. Note the ancient oak pollards (*Quercus*), gnarled bark and dead wood – useful evidence for centuries-old woodland management at Ickworth.[3]

Overleaf: An oak tree (*Quercus*) in winter at Ickworth: 'I wonder if the snow loves the trees and fields, that it kisses them so gently? And then it covers them up snug, you know, with a white quilt; and perhaps it says "Go to sleep, darlings, till the summer comes again".' (Quoted from *Alice through the Looking Glass*)[4]

The Tea Party Oak (*Quercus robur*) takes on a sculptural aspect during the winter months.

known as the 'mini Ice Age', as well as the depopulation of England caused by an epidemic of the Great Plague. As the tree entered the eighteenth century it began its gradual yet graceful demise. Oaks start to decline when they are around 600 years old: first the crown recedes creating a stag-headed appearance, the trunk continues to broaden and hollow, and the bark becomes much coarser and more deeply furrowed.

Many of the trees and woodlands at Ickworth are still recovering from the effects of the Second World War when, in an effort to 'dig for victory' and to become more self-sufficient in providing food, land was cleared so that potatoes and other staple crops could be planted. Fortunately, the Tea Party Oak and upwards of 200 other ancient and veteran trees have survived, providing habitats on which rare invertebrates, mosses and lichens continue to depend. It is for this reason that Ickworth is recognised as internationally important for wildlife. Most of the very old trees at Ickworth are oaks and are considered ecosystems in their own right, some supporting over 300 different species.

The weather-beaten Tea Party Oak is an awe-inspiring tree. Against all the odds it has remained determinedly rooted to the spot while more than 30 human generations have passed. It provides a tangible link to our history and has acted as an island of stability that has enabled micro-organisms from the eleventh century, the time of the Normans, to survive through to today.

The Biblical cedars

In 1795 Frederick Augustus, 4th Earl of Bristol, initiated the construction of the magnificent buildings that we see at Ickworth. At the same time a number of cedar of Lebanon trees (*Cedrus libani*) were planted to shield the construction site from view. Once established these elegant trees became part of the garden and the plan to remove them once the building was completed was abandoned. It was agreed that the house should be hidden from the visitors' view until the

King Hiram of Tyre brings men to help the Israelites cut cedar trees to rebuild the temple of Solomon in Jerusalem, hand-coloured woodcut of a nineteenth-century illustration.

The cedars of Lebanon (*Cedrus libani*) that were originally planted to screen the construction work on the rotunda have grown into fine trees.

very last moment, when they would be presented with a surprise landscape: the cedars' feathery outlines framing the splendid rotunda.

In Biblical times, cedars of Lebanon formed an almost unbroken forest from Israel to Turkey. However, a great many were felled during the construction of buildings such as the well-known 'Temple of Solomon' in Jerusalem. In the Old Testament there are records of the extraordinary volumes of cedar wood harvested and the labour required for such a huge project. The result was that most of the cedar forests in the Middle East disappeared more than 2,000 years ago, although in two protected areas in Lebanon there remain small numbers of ancient cedars that are believed to be over 1,000 years old.

1. Rackham 2006, p. 56.
2. Ibid., p. 58.
3. Forrest 2014, p. 10.
4. Carroll 1872, p. 4.

Kedleston Hall

Derbyshire

The parkland that surrounds the large lake and grand house at Kedleston is home to one of the finest collections of ancient and veteran trees in the Midlands. A classic historic British deer park, small groups of sheep can be seen grazing under the spreading boughs of great ash (*Fraxinus excelsior*) and oak (*Quercus*) trees, some of which are many hundreds of years old. But not all is as it seems.

The hollowing trunk of an ancient ash pollard (*Fraxinus excelsior*) provides habitats for a number of rare invertebrates.

On delving briefly into the history of Kedleston it soon becomes apparent that it is a 'designed' landscape, which is contrived and artificial. Landscape architect Robert Adam completely transformed the estate in the eighteenth century.

The lake is man-made and Adam redesigned and landscaped the entire grounds by constructing undulations that previously did not exist. For almost a decade thousands of tons of earth were moved by men wielding shovels and using horses and carts to achieve the effect seen today. By ingeniously allowing the ancient and veteran trees to remain, probably for aesthetic reasons, Adam managed to retain the traditional deer park appearance of the grounds, while inadvertently creating islands of biological continuity within the man-made parkland. Today Kedleston is one of the top locations in Britain – because of the sheer variety of insects – for rare invertebrates living on ageing trees. It is hard to imagine the environmental consequences if the ancient and veteran trees had been removed at the time of the redevelopment.

Ancient islands

Ancient and dead trees support many more types of wildlife than young trees and are particularly important to what are known as saproxylic invertebrates – beetles, hoverflies, moths, spiders, false scorpions and snails – which rely on decaying wood. Ancient trees are vital to those organisms that spend their larval stages in rotting wood, such as stag beetles (*Lucanus cervus*), whose larvae live for six years within the wood before they pupate and emerge as adults. The adult's life is a mere four months. Even the quality of dead wood changes over time and each stage of decay can provide a variety of habitats for different specialist invertebrates. Some insects

One of the horse chestnuts (*Aesculus hippocastanum*) at Kedleston Hall is an excellent example of what is often referred to as a 'walking tree'.

thrive on wood that is slightly decayed whereas others, such as death-watch beetles (*Xestobium rufovillosum*), click beetles (*sp. Elateridae* listed in the *Red Data Book*) and many types of fly, feed only on wood that has been almost completely broken down by fungi. Another *Red Data Book* species found at Kedleston is the oak polypore fungus (*Piptoporus quercinus*), which depends on the decaying heartwood of oak trees that are at least 250 years old.

Different species of fungi create different types of decayed wood: the common southern bracket (*Ganoderma australe*) causes a spongy wet white rot, while chicken of the woods (*Laetiporus sulphureus*) and beefsteak (*Fistulina hepatica*) produce the rarer dry brittle brown or red cubical rot, each with their associated fauna. The white rot fungi consume lignin, which gives wood its strength and rigidity, while leaving the white cellulose untouched. Red rot, on the other hand, digests the cellulose that provides the wood's flexibility, and the retained lignin produces the characteristic red cubes. Dead wood supplies the hunting grounds for species that prey on invertebrates associated with old trees, like parasitic wasps, and larger animals such as birds and bats.

In order to retain the extraordinary biodiversity found at Kedleston it is important that the ancient trees are carefully managed and that trees of various ages are also present in the park, not only to provide additional habitats but also to create continuity by eventually replacing the old trees of today. Looking after these special old trees is a science that is still under development. However, it is known that not only do the fallen limbs left to decay around the bases of trees increase biodiversity, but they also keep the destructive feet of sheep away from their roots, thereby preventing physical damage and soil compaction.

Kedleston is an outstanding example of how an almost entirely man-made landscape can still be hugely beneficial to wildlife, particularly if its ancient trees are managed properly.

A large ancient oak pollard (*Quercus*) complete with oak apples in May.

Killerton
Devon

An enormous giant redwood tree (*Sequoiadendron giganteum*), also called Wellingtonia, which was among the very first to be planted in England.

In many ways Killerton is a living time capsule. Left to the National Trust in 1944 the country estate is unusual in having retained so many of its eighteenth-century features. At its heart the house is surrounded by ornamental gardens and what is considered to be one of the first arboretums in Britain, a living testament to the great plant collectors who brought back new exotic species from all parts of the world.

Much of what can be seen at Killerton, particularly with regard to trees, is the result of the handiwork of the talented nurseryman and landscape designer John Veitch and his descendants. The 19-year-old Veitch arrived at Killerton in 1770 and was tasked by Sir Thomas Dyke Acland, 7th Baronet of Killerton, at first to help with, but soon after to be in charge of, the design of a new garden and landscape. Sir Acland's plan was to create the splendid sweeping vistas across manicured gardens and the extensive parkland that was fashionable at the time and admired by visitors today.

An ancient oak (*Quercus*) with a great hollow trunk, which provides nesting opportunities for a variety of birds and habitats for specialist invertebrates that feed on dead wood.

Rising up to the north of the main house is Dolbury Hill, an Iron Age hill fort built on an extinct volcano. Over the last 200 years the south-facing slopes of the hill, affectionately known as the 'Clump', have been extensively planted with both native and exotic tree species in order to provide the grand backdrop to the main house.

Redwoods

The volcanic hill contains fine examples of the giant sequoia, or redwood trees (*Sequoiadendron giganteum*). The oldest of these magnificent monoliths is believed to have been the very first redwood in England to have been grown from seed in 1843. However, the largest redwood in the garden today is actually one that was planted a few years later, in 1858; it is 37 metres tall and has a girth of 6.55 metres. Millions of years ago redwoods were among the commonest trees in the northern hemisphere. The giant redwood forests are now restricted to the Sierra Nevada's western slopes in California, USA, where the biggest tree ever recorded, known as the General Sherman, stands 83.8 metres tall, with a girth of 31.1 metres. The redwoods at Killerton are already among the tallest trees in Britain, but in theory they could live for another 2,000 years and double their height.

A view across the park towards the main house at Killerton.

The trunks of a young silver birch (*Betula pendula*) and an ancient hawthorn (*Crataegus monogyna*) fused at the base.

Deodar cedar

In the wild the Deodar cedar (*Cedrus deodara*) is found in parts of northern Pakistan, Afghanistan, Kashmir, India and Nepal along the foothills of the Himalayas. The name 'Deodar' is believed to come from the Sanskrit *devadaru*, which means 'tree of the gods', an apt name for such stunning specimens. Killerton was the first garden in Britain in which a deodar cedar set seed, and many of the deodar cedars in Park Wood on the estate are likely to be its progeny.

Air tree

On the summit of the Clump, just beyond the main planted area of native and non-native trees, is a small grassy field in which can be found a most unusual double tree. From a distance it looks like a young silver birch (*Betula pendula*) but on closer inspection you can see that the birch is actually growing directly out of an ancient hawthorn (*Crataegus monogyna*). Rather than being single entities the two trees have grown and fused together. Many years ago the ancient hawthorn's decaying heartwood became exposed. A birch seed opportunistically landed on the decaying wood, germinated and took root, creating this unusual structure. Trees that grow on and out of other trees are often referred to as 'air trees' or 'bird trees' depending on how the seed was deposited. Birches are particularly good air trees as they are excellent colonisers. They were one of the first trees to become established after the last Ice Age because their seeds were light in weight and easily dispersed by the wind.

A felled giant redwood tree (*Sequoiadendron giganteum*) in California in 1917, which gives an idea of their enormous size.

Kingston Lacy
Dorset

The house and grounds of Kingston Lacy are located close to the town of Wimborne Minster in a part of the country that is believed to have been continuously farmed for more than 5,000 years. A striking feature of the estate is Badbury Rings, a large Iron Age earthwork dating from 800 BC. It comprises three concentric circular banks with a sanctuary at its heart. Nearly 3,000 years after its construction it still remains a significant mark on the Dorset landscape. One of the eighteenth-century occupants of Kingston Lacy left an equally prominent mark in the form of one of the finest beech (*Fagus sylvatica*) avenues in England, and possibly the most loved; it is admired by thousands of people daily.

William John Bankes was a notorious character. He spent little time at his family seat at Kingston Lacy preferring to

The beech (*Fagus sylvatica*) avenue at Kingston Lacy comprised 366 trees on one side of the road and 365 trees on the other when it was planted, creating a lasting mark on the Dorset landscape.

A view across the park to the north front of the house.

travel, collect art, mix with high society and lead a life of excitement. While he was at Cambridge University he met and became great friends with the poet George Gordon Noel, 6th Baron Byron. Byron, who was no stranger to travel and having a good time himself, felt almost upstaged by his friend, famously describing him in a letter to John Murray in 1820 as 'the father of all mischiefs'.[1]

In 1835 Bankes returned to Kingston Lacy and planted the spectacular avenue of beech (*Fagus sylvatica*) in memory of his mother. Rather than a modest avenue leading to the house, his was more in keeping with his flamboyant personality and stretched for 4 kilometres (2.5 miles) along the turnpike between Blandford Forum and Wimborne Minster. When planted, it comprised 365 trees on one side of the road and 366 on the other, and in autumn and spring its beauty is breathtaking. Despite their age, over 500 of the trees survive; a second avenue has recently been planted behind the original, to eventually replace it.

When walking along the majestic avenue it is possible to see the occasional tree that has a much more splayed root plate than the others. This broad grey flange of extra growth, with its claw-like projections spreading from the base, gives the appearance that the tree is almost trying to grip the ground. In many respects this is exactly what the tree is doing (see also Dunham Massey, p. 64).

Within the parkland at Kingston Lacy there are many impressive stumpy and twisted old trees. Of particular interest is a stunning ancient holm or holly oak (*Quercus ilex*), one of the most characterful examples of the species in Britain. The tree's leaves are similar to those of holly; *holm* is the ancient name for holly and in Latin it is *Ilex*. Holm oaks were introduced into Britain in the sixteenth century and are native to the Mediterranean region. Nearby there is another tree more naturally found around the Mediterranean: a fine old sweet chestnut (*Castanea sativa*) in the process of becoming shorter and fatter with age.

1. Elledge 2000, p. 147.

The trees in the avenue are all reaching an age that is considered ancient for beech (*Fagus sylvatica*).

Knole
Kent

Knole, near to Sevenoaks, has been a deer park for more than 400 years.[1] The park and the town were famed for their wonderful trees and especially the oaks (*Quercus robur* and *Q. petraea*). Sadly the great storm of 1987 blew over six of the seven oaks in the town and around 70 per cent of the trees at Knole. However, there are still many fine old trees to be seen.

The park was nationally famous for hundreds of years for its spectacular large and ancient trees. A map created in 1898 shows the locations of the most well-known trees at the time: the 'King Beech', the 'Old Oak' and the 'King John Oak'. The 'Old Oak' (or the 'Witches Tree') was reputed to be both the tallest and oldest of its species in the park in 1895. A monstrous multi-stemmed beech (*Fagus sylvatica*), called the 'King Beech', was immortalised in postcards, including those produced by the renowned Victorian photographer Francis Frith. The 'King John Oak' was said to have been used as a hiding place by the king when he was being pursued. All three trees were so magnificent that were regularly referred to in historic writings:

> *Knole park* is on a higher site, more varied in surface, and even more beautiful than Penshurst. It is very extensive, abundantly stocked with deer, and richly wooded. The *beeches* are perhaps hardly elsewhere to be equalled for number, size, health, and beauty ... Not far from it is a very large *oak*, said by Mr. Brady to have been known two centuries ago as 'The Old Oak'.[2]

Ancient trees are particularly robust. With their broad, squat and hollow trunks, along with their reduced canopies, very few succumb to winter storms. Depressingly, the most common cause of their destruction since Victorian times has been fire. The King's Oak was destroyed by arsonists in 1950 and the same fate befell the Witches Oak in 1954. More than 60 years after the demise of the last of the three great trees of Knole, they continue to exist in the collective memory of local people.

In addition to the 'ghost trees' of Knole there is reputed to be at least one ghost – that of Lady Anne Gifford, wife of the disreputable Black Night, Richard Sackville – who wanders among the oaks of Duchess Walk at night.

Knole is famed not only for its beetles but also for The Beatles, who shot a pioneering promotional film for their song 'Strawberry Fields Forever' on the estate in 1967, using a decaying ancient oak as their backdrop.

Woodcut of the Old Oak (*Quercus*), which was destroyed by lightning in 1764.

The Old Oak (*Quercus*), or Witches Tree, at the beginning of the twentieth century.

The west front of the house at Knole through the spreading branches of a 300-year-old sycamore (*Acer pseudoplatanus*).

The oak in literature

There are many references to oaks in literature. In Homer's *Odyssey* (8th century BC), Odysseus travelled to a famous oak at Dodona, in north-west Greece, to find out from its 'lofty foliage' the plans of Zeus. The tree was reputed to be such a height that one could spy on the gods from the top. In Virginia Woolf's novel *Orlando* (1928) – a thinly veiled love letter to Vita Sackville West and based on Knole – a character is described as climbing 'to a place crowned by a single oak tree', a tree so remarkably tall that they could see not only the spires of London and the ships of the Armada at sea but even the peaks of Snowdon and the tides of the Hebrides.

1. Taylor 2003, pp. 153–84.
2. Knight *et al.* 1847–51, p. 22.

Lanhydrock

Cornwall

Situated around 5 kilometres (3 miles) south of Bodmin and covering 360 hectares, Lanhydrock is one of the most important sites in Britain for lichens thanks to its fine collection of ancient and veteran trees. In medieval times, Lanhydrock, meaning 'church enclosure of St Hydrock', was a monastic farm feeding the Augustinian monks at the priory in Bodmin. Following the Dissolution of the Monasteries in the late 1530s, it was eventually acquired by Sir Richard Robartes in 1620 and remained in the family until being given to the National Trust in 1953. Lanhydrock's garden, famous for its stunning collection of rhododendron, azaleas and especially magnolias of which there are over 120 species, is protected from the prevailing south-westerly winds coming off the Atlantic by extensive woodlands, creating a sheltered microclimate.

The park

Unlike many of its contemporaries the beautifully laid out parkland was never formally designed; instead it slowly evolved. Shortly after the Dissolution it became a deer park, which over the centuries expanded and contracted along with the family's fortunes and their whims. Thankfully the old trees were kept by the successive generations and new trees added to produce the fine landscape seen today.

The incredible number of lichen species, over 130 recorded to date, is in part due to the climate in the damp south-west, but crucially it is a reflection of the long continuous presence of ancient trees within the park and across the estate. Many lichen species, particularly the rarest, are extremely poor travellers. They require sufficient numbers of suitable old open-grown trees to be able to move from one to another over hundreds of years.

One of the many great oaks (*Quercus*), complete with a large burr, that grace the parkland at Lanhydrock.

The estate is also a national hotspot for its bat community. While approximately 20 per cent of all mammal species worldwide are bats, in Britain the 17 resident species make up over 25 per cent. Thirteen have been recorded at Lanhydrock, including the rare greater horseshoe (*Rhinolophus ferrumequinum*) and barbastelle (*Barbastella barbastellus*) bats. Most British bats require old trees, either as roosting sites within hollow trunks and split limbs or as places from which to feed on the invertebrates flying around at night. Greater horseshoe bats favour open parkland where they feed above grazing cattle.

The avenue

A grand double beech (*Fagus sylvatica*) avenue runs from the house for about 850 metres east to the edge of the park and what was the historic main entrance at Lanhydrock. It was first planted in 1657 as a single sycamore (*Acer pseudoplatanus*) avenue, possible to commemorate the Parliamentary victory in the Civil War. The Robartes family was unusual for Cornwall, where most of the gentry were Royalists.

The gate house and ornamental gardens that surround the main house.

The parkland is rich in fallen and decaying wood, which provides habitats for many different types of rare invertebrates.

In the 1820s the avenue underwent a dramatic change when the original was replaced with two rows of beech trees on either side of the drive. The avenue today retains several old and hollow sycamore trees within the inner two beech rows, which could be from the earliest planting, but their small size makes this difficult to believe. It is quite possible that these sycamore had been replacement plantings just prior to the doubling of the avenue and were thus spared the axe. There are also a couple of oaks (*Quercus*) at the lower end of the avenue, which are historic parkland trees that pre-date the avenue, but were in ideal locations to be incorporated into the formal planting.

Pymouth pear

At first glance the Plymouth pear tree (*Pyrus cordata*) does not look particularly special. It has small spherical marble-sized fruit about 1.3 centimetres in diameter and rather thin prickly branches that make it more reminiscent of a blackthorn than a pear tree. However, it is one of the rarest trees in Britain. There are only two genetically distinct trees known to exist in the wild: one, located in Plymouth where it was first recorded in 1870, has an upright form, and the other, near Truro, is more pendulous. The rest of the surrounding populations of both are clones of these two mother trees, which over the years have reproduced and spread by producing suckers.

The delicate flower of the extremely rare Plymouth pear (*Pyrus cordata*).

The natural range of the species is along the Atlantic coastal zone from Brittany in France down through Spain and Portugal and along the north Mediterranean coast to Algeria. It is not known whether the trees in Plymouth and Truro are remnants of a pre-glacial population, or if they arrived in Britain having been transported by birds or were introduced as hedging material hundreds of years ago.

An English Nature (now Natural England) Species Recovery Project based at Lanhydrock was established in 1995 to try and save the unique biodiversity of the Plymouth pear. This involved the controlled cross-pollination of the two forms, taking male flowers from Truro to pollinate the Plymouth female flower, and from the male Plymouth to the female Truro, in order to get a viable seed from which the next generation of trees can develop.

Lanhydrock was chosen as the site for the project for several reasons. Firstly, it is an equal distance from the two natural populations. Secondly, the remote heathland area on the edge of the estate has very similar conditions and soils to those where the pear grows wild in Brittany. Thirdly, it was felt that locating the project on National Trust land would give it long-term security. And finally, it was isolated enough from domestic pear trees to prevent the trees hybridising with commercial specimens. In total ten groups of six trees were planted within fenced enclosures, each group containing all of the possible variations within such a limited population. The young trees are currently doing very well.

Melford Hall

Suffolk

Melford Hall, the country seat of the Hyde Parker family, is located on the edge of the large village of Long Melford. Surrounding the main house are exquisitely manicured ornamental gardens planted with exotic plants, trees and shrubs.

On the lawn to the west of the house stands a wonderful black mulberry tree (*Morus nigra*). It is huge and sprawling and has taken on the recumbent form typical to ancient mulberries. Beneath its large dome of glossy green leaves it has the most beautifully contorted trunk and limbs. It is almost as if it has become slightly fed up with gravity and has decided to loll on its woody elbows and knees. It is considered to be over 400 years old, which is possibly true because many of the landed gentry who attended the court of King James I in the early 1600s were encouraged to plant mulberries (the leaves of which provide food for silkworms) in an attempt to help stimulate Britain's own silk industry. Unfortunately the wrong mulberry was imported: the silkworms feed on white mulberry (*Morus alba*), not the black variety.

The mulberry and the silk industry

The white mulberry can grow reasonably well in southern Britain, but it is susceptible to hard frost. After the failure of

An ancient mulberry tree (*Morus nigra*) on the lawn to the west of the main house at Melford Hall.

Opposite: *Map of Little Park, Melford Hall, Long Melford,* by Samuel Pierse, 1613 (detail).
This unique painting of the Melford Hall estate, with its unusual tree-mounted hunting platforms and hides, hangs in a private area of the main house.

the black mulberry experiment, few of the white variety were planted and the silk was imported. Around 1685 more than 500,000 Huguenots left France after persecution by King Louis XIV, many of whom settled in the East End of London with the blessing of one of their great allies, King James II. A hundred years later, after creating an affluent cartel in London, the capital's judges tried to regulate the Huguenots' wealth and industry. The result was that a great number headed east out of London arriving in Haverhill, Sudbury and Glemsford in the early 1780s, which happily coincided with a time when the working class in Suffolk was desperate for employment. By 1844 there were four silk manufacturers and some 600 silk looms in Sudbury, just a short distance from Melford Hall.

The deer and the tree houses

In 1613, Samuel Pierse painted a wonderful and enormous work, which hangs in the private quarters of the main house at Melford Hall. The painting depicts a number of large oaks (*Quercus*) on the Melford estate with structures among them, known as 'standings', from which hunters were able to shoot deer with bows and arrows. While the classic image of deer hunting is *par force* – that is, men on horseback and hounds in hot pursuit of a stag – this was rare because most deer parks in Britain were not large enough to accommodate this style of hunt. There were a variety of practices employed in the small- and medium- sized parks, including 'bow and stable' as shown in Pierse's painting. This is where a line of men (the 'stable') would encourage the herd of deer to move towards the 'standing' where they could be shot cleanly. One of the main advantages of the 'bow and stable' hunt was that it could be carried out throughout the year (apart from in the 'fence', or breeding, month) and in deer parks of all sizes. In the painting two 'standings', both two storeys high, can be seen. The upper storey was for spectators so they could watch the hunt from close quarters.

The history of Melford Hall and the grounds

The history of Melford Hall and the trees in the grounds that surround it follows a pattern that is typical of similar properties. Before the Norman invasion of 1066, the estate was run by the Church – in this case the Benedictine monastery at Bury St Edmunds. At this time, the trees would have formed part of a 'working' forest landscape providing timber for building, wood for fuel and brash for animal fodder.

An ancient stag-headed oak (*Quercus*) showing many of the features of an ancient tree, including dead wood in the canopy and a broad trunk.

After the Dissolution of the Monasteries King Henry VIII generally installed his own tenants in the properties he acquired from the Church. At Melford Hall it was William Cordell, who took over in 1547. The king and his associates were particularly interested in hunting, although this would have had little effect on the large trees and managed forests of the time. Eventually, after the bankruptcy of the then owner Lady Rivers, Sir Harry Parker, 6th Baronet, bought Melford in 1768. The Hyde Parkers have been in residence ever since and the current occupant is the 12th Baronet, Sir Richard Hyde Parker.

During the Hyde Parker dynasty there have been many changes to the trees and woodlands on the estate, the most profound of which were related to the Acts of Enclosure during the eighteenth and nineteenth centuries. This was the legal process by which open fields or commons could be enclosed and the property rights given to an individual. Between 1760 and 1820 the enclosures across Britain resulted in local people loing their common rights, so creating a landless working class that could be exploited by the new industries at the beginning of the Industrial Revolution.

At Melford the traditional forest management would have changed and the strip fields of individual families combined into larger paddocks and fields ringed by hawthorn hedges. While the typical fate of the forests after enclosure according to Oliver Rackham was that the 'private owners instantly destroyed them', the owners of Melford Hall were more benign. Even though the landscape was enclosed and 'designed', many of the magnificent ancient oak trees seen in the 1613 painting still survive in a private corner of the estate, along with their extraordinarily rich biodiversity.

Morden Hall Park
London

Once considered to be in the wilds of Surrey, the green oasis that is Morden Hall Park has now been swallowed up by the urban sprawl of Greater London.

Morden Hall Park is an important area for many Londoners because it gives them a chance to escape the hustle and bustle of the city and to experience more natural surroundings. The park is bisected by the meandering River Wandle, lined with water-loving trees, typically willow (*Salix*) and alder (*Alnus*). However, there is also an unusual veteran corkscrew willow (*Salix matsudana* 'Tortuosa') with long contorted leaves and a hollow decaying trunk. These trees provide the habitat for many insects, which in turn are prey to dragonflies, and roosting sites for birds like herons (*Ardea cinerea*) and kingfishers (*Alcedo atthis*). The park is also home to mature oak (*Quercus*) and elm (*Ulmus*) trees that were mostly planted in avenues in the eighteenth and nineteenth centuries. There is a small arboretum where a number of exotic trees can be seen, notably one wonderfully gnarled mulberry tree (*Morus nigra*), which is tipped over at a jaunty angle and is thought to be around 400 years old. The first mulberry tree to be planted in London was at Syon Park in 1548.

An ancient black mulberry (*Morus nigra*) leaning in a way typical to old mulberries.

Trees and health

In 1984 the researcher Roger Ulrich showed that hospital patients could recover more rapidly from surgical procedures if there was a 'green' view from either their hospital or home windows.[1] His work stimulated urban planners and medics to look into the health benefits that trees provide in cities.

It is estimated that there are around 8 million trees in London today, which line the streets and thrive in parks such as at Morden Hall. Rather than being seen as purely decorative they have now been shown to be worth millions of pounds annually for the important environmental services they provide and the associated improvements in health that they bring.[2] The trees remove air

A kingfisher (*Acedo atthis*).

A ringlet butterfly (*Aphantopus hyperantus*), one of the many butterfly species that can be seen in the park.

pollution, retain rain water and effectively 'air condition' the city by ameliorating extreme highs and lows of temperature. The presence of trees in populated areas has also been proven to reduce the incidence of asthma, to improve the development of unborn babies and to have positive effects on the general psychological welfare of the local population.

Since 2008, Boris Johnson, Mayor of London, has organised the planting of more than 20,000 trees. However, while trees of any age in urban areas help improve air quality and reduce flash flooding, mature and ancient trees in parks such as that at Morden Hall have been shown to have far greater environmental and wildlife benefits than young trees.

1. Ulrich 1984, pp. 420–21.
2. If every household in England was provided with good access to quality green space it could save an estimated £2.1 billion in health care costs. 'Our National Health Service – the role of the natural environment in maintaining healthy lives', Natural England 2009, www.naturalengland.org.uk/publications, accessed July 2015.
3. Columbia University researchers found asthma rates among children aged four and five fell by a quarter for every 343 trees per square kilometre. Lovasi *et al.* 2008, pp. 647–49.

The parkland with a fine avenue of lime trees (*Tilia*) and large open-grown oaks (*Quercus*) provides a welcome location for Londoners to relax.

Mottisfont
Hampshire

Founded in 1201 as an Augustinian priory, Mottisfont Abbey boasts some spectacular ancient and veteran trees within its extensive grounds. When the priory was dissolved in 1536, it was given to William Sandys, King Henry VIII's lord chamberlain, who converted the buildings into a house. The property eventually descended to the Mill family who changed its name from 'priory' to 'abbey'. They created hunting and fishing lodges and enhanced the gardens by planting sweet chestnuts (*Castanea sativa*), London planes (*Plantinus x acerifolia*) and avenues of lime (*Tilia*). The trees added to an estate already rich in oaks (*Quercus*), many of which were fully grown in the Middle Ages.

The south front of Mottisfont Abbey.

Opposite: The trunk of the Great London Plane (*Platanus x acerifolia*) is over 11.8 metres in girth.

The Oakley Oak (*Quercus robur*), which stands on the banks of the River Test, is one of the largest and oldest oak trees in Hampshire.

The Oakley Oak

Located at the very furthest north-east extent of the grounds is one of the grandest and largest oaks at Mottisfont. It is known as the 'Oakley Oak' (*Quercus robur*) and has a gigantic girth of 10.74 metres. It displays the classic shape of an oak tree that has been pollarded for many centuries and now has a huge squat trunk and a low, spreading crown supported on a network of branches that sprout from a base some 2.5 metres above the ground. Oak trees with girths in excess of 10 metres are considered to be around 1,000 years old. It is likely, therefore, that the Oakley Oak is older than the Abbey ruins. Its name also supports this theory with O/E *leah* meaning 'a clearing in woodland'.

The Great London Plane

Larger than the Oakley Oak, the 'Great London Plane' (*Platanus x acerifolia*) has a girth of 11.8 metres and a height

The Napoleon Crab Apple (*Malus sylvestris*) sits on the northern lawn and is one of the most ancient fruit trees in Britain.

approaching 40 metres. London plane trees are believed to be a hybrid of the oriental (*Platanus orientalis*) and the North American plane species (*Platanus occidentalis*), which were initially observed in southern Europe in the mid-seventeenth century. The first record of a London plane (originally known as a Spanish plane) being planted in Britain is around 1680. It is believed that the Great London Plane was planted between 1722 and 1742 during the tenure of the Mill family at Mottisfont, which would give it an age of about 280 years.

The Napoleon Crab Apple

Not only an ancient tree for its type, the Napoleon Crab Apple (*Malus sylvestris*) also provides a fascinating link between Mottisfont and Napoleon Bonaparte's incarceration on St Helena in the Atlantic Ocean. Napolean's gaoler on the island, Sir Hudson Lowe, was a friend of the Revd John Barker-Mill of Mottisfont. Lowe had few friends in England after his return from St Helena in 1821 other than the Barker-Mill family largely because Dr Barry O'Meara, Napoleon's doctor on St Helena, had surreptitiously published *The Opinions and Reflections of Napoleon* in July 1822.[1] In the book Lowe was portrayed in a poor light and was implicated in the supposed mistreatment of Napoleon and his subsequent premature death. It is uncertain whether the accusations were true or whether the surgeon was being bribed by Napoleon and his supporters (something that had helped facilitate Napoleon's previous escape from Elba) but the effect was that Lowe was virtually excommunicated from British society. He had hoped that the establishment would support his view of events but he was shunned and never even gained the pension that his title merited.

As a souvenir of his time on St Helena, Lowe is said to have brought back crab apples to Mottisfont where he planted one on the north lawn in front of the main house, at the end of an avenue of pleached lime trees (*Tilia*). The crab apple is undoubtedly old because it is shown as a mature tree in an aerial photograph taken in 1938. A planting date of 1821–22 would appear to be entirely possible considering its size and condition both now and in the photograph. Two hundred years old is a great age for a crab apple and would make it one of the oldest of its species in Britain.

1. O'Meara 1822.

Blossom on the Napoleon Crab Apple tree (*Malus sylvestris*).

Petworth House and Park

West Sussex

The house and Upper Pond at Petworth.

Petworth House is surrounded by a great park that covers 238 hectares. It has a fine collection of ancient trees, Britain's largest herd of fallow deer and many grand vistas. The origins of the park date back to over 1,000 years ago and it was known to have been visited regularly by King Henry VIII in the sixteenth century, which is not hard to imagine while walking among the old trees. When the park became crown property in 1537 the king had a banqueting hall constructed on Arbor Hill from which he could watch the horse riders and dogs in pursuit of the deer. Today the park bears the unmistakable stamp of the landscape designer Capability Brown, who worked on the estate between 1751 and 1763. It is also immortalised by the romantic landscape painter Joseph Mallord William Turner.

Close to the northern edge of the park there are not only exotic species such as southern beech (*Nothofagus*) from Chile growing in among native trees but also the curiously named Beelzebub Oak (*Quercus*). It has its own plaque and has even given its name to the bus stop on the other side of the perimeter wall. The oak was a former boundary maker and is shown on the map that formed part of James Crow's survey of the Petworth estate in 1779. On the western edge of the park, growing up against the wall, is a particularly unusual 'walking tree', a grey poplar (*Populus x canescens*), which is a hybrid between white poplar (*Populus alba*) and common aspen (*Populus tremula*). The trunk has lost some of its rigidity due to fungal decay, causing it to gradually lean over until it finally touched the ground, reminiscent of a candle drooping in the hot sun. Once the trunk touches the soil it sends down roots and another tree is formed. The process can be repeated many times enabling the tree to slowly 'walk' across the ground over the centuries (see also Blickling, p. 27).

In the heart of the park stand some impressive burred oaks many of which tower over the pasture around them. The largest pedunculate oak (*Quercus robur*) has a girth of 9 metres indicating that it is around 700 to 800 years old. The grandest sessile oak (*Quercus petraea*) is slightly more than 7 metres around the trunk and could be over 500 years of age. Possibly

The ancient small-leaved lime (*Tilia cordata*) coppice stool set high on the rise in front of the lake may be over 1,000 years old.

A huge oak (*Quercus*) with a girth of over 8 metres, which was already old when Capability Brown was landscaping Petworth Park.

The Lake, Petworth: Sunset, Fighting Bucks, *c*.1829, by Joseph Mallord William Turner (1775–1851).

the oldest tree is an ancient small-leaved lime (*Tilia cordata*). It is easy to walk right past it because it is in a state of collapse. Over time fungal decay has passed from the ripe wood at the centre of the tree through to the living wood and right out through the bark. This does not mean that the tree is dying, but that with great age it has divided itself into several discrete functional units effectively creating a number of independent trees. There are also many large sweet chestnuts (*Castanea sativa*) in the park, a favourite tree of Capability Brown.

Capability Brown and Joseph Mallord William Turner

A visitor to the magnificent parkland that surrounds Petworth House has the opportunity to almost step back in time by gazing across views created by Capability Brown and painted by Turner. A walk uphill to the north-west away from the main lake takes you to the very spot where Turner painted *The Lake, Petworth: Sunset, Fighting Bucks* around 1829. The painting almost glows yellow with its sunset colouring the sky beyond and a herd of fallow deer grazing in the foreground. The small copse of trees at the top right of the painting still exists nearly 200 years later as do the lime avenues and sweet chestnuts close to the lake. The main absentees from the scene are the lofty elms (*Ulmus*), lost to Dutch elm disease, which would have formerly graced the landscape. A phenomenally successful painter who enjoyed great wealth while he was still

Petworth has a collection of mature exotic trees such as this southern beech (*Nothofagus*).

alive, Turner was a good friend of the owner of Petworth House, 3rd Earl of Egremont, and today the 20 works held at Petworth represent the largest single collection of Turner canvases outside Tate Britain.

Capability Brown, though not as sympathetic towards very old trees as the other great landscape designer Humphry Repton, nevertheless included a number of ancient specimens in his landscaped vistas. He is reputed to have left the oldest sweet chestnuts untouched and planted many more for their aesthetic qualities, either standing alone or in avenues. The trees that Brown planted will themselves become the ancients of the future.

The remarkable 'walking' grey poplar (*Populus x canescens*) appears to be zig-zagging across the ground on the far west boundary of the park.

Plas Newydd
Anglesey

Plas Newydd is near to Llanfairpwllgwyngyll, on the island of Anglesey, and situated on the banks of the Menai Strait with magnificent views across to Snowdonia. It is the seat of the Marquess of Anglesey and was acquired by the National Trust in 1976. The house originates from the fourteenth century but has been expanded over the years and was significantly altered in the eighteenth century by the architect James Wyatt, a rival to his more famous contemporary Robert Adams. The National Trust has recently invested £600,000 in a marine source heating pump that will produce 300 kilowatts of electricity, the largest in Britain and expected to save around £40,000 per year in energy costs.

The estate consists of 68 hectares of parkland, gardens and woodland all containing some rather special trees, which you first experience when parking your car among the elegant sycamores (*Acer pseudoplatanus*). In the south-east section of the garden is a remarkable ancient oak (*Quercus*), about 600 years old, whose trunk is split down the middle. Extensive heartwood decay had weakened the remaining shell and the weight of the crown caused the split. Subsequently, work was carried out to reduce the weight by trimming the crown. The tree has responded well and looks likely to live another few hundred years.

Another magnificent tree is the sycamore located on the edge of the garden, which is referred to as Repton's Pollard. In 1799 the great landscape architect Humphry Repton completed a commission for Plas Newydd, but sadly only the text from his report survives. It is thought that the sycamore was pollarded as part of Repton's vision for the parkland. He was associated with the Picturesque movement and liked to create vistas towards architectural features in the distance, which included interesting trees. This may be the explanation for the pollarding of this sycamore.

The beech

Within the woodland is a beech (*Fagus sylvatica*) that is truly breathtaking in size. It has a colossal girth of 10.55 metres at a height of 1 metre. It looks as though it is several trees fused together. It may actually be an old hedgerow tree that was cut

The multi-stemmed tree set on the edge of a quarry at Plas Newydd is a beech (*Fagus sylvatica*) with the largest trunk in Britain, with a girth of over 10 metres.

A wonderful 400-year-old oak (*Quercus*) with a beautifully splayed base to its trunk and with a girth of nearly 8 metres.

at ground level a couple of hundred years ago and re-grew the multiple stems that we see now. However it was formed, it is indeed a giant of a tree.

Beech at risk

The predictions for Britain's future climate are that we will experience hotter, drier summers and an increase in the number of severe weather events. This is not good news for Britain's beeches, which have very shallow roots so making them prone to drought stress and wind-throw. Beech is the tree most commonly blown over by extreme winds. Does this mean the demise of British beeches? If these predictions prove to be accurate, existing mature beeches will certainly suffer. However, beeches are found in some very hot, dry regions of Europe, such as the Dordogne in France and Sicily in Italy. Therefore, hopefully many of the young seedlings growing up in Britain during this period of climate change will be resilient enough to adapt to these circumstances by sending out deeper roots to seek more reliable moisture and stable soil conditions, which will provide an improved anchor.

Repton planted and instantly pollarded a number of sycamore trees (*Acer pseudoplatanus*) at Plas Newydd in order to encourage the canopy to spread widely.

Scotney Castle
Kent

The ruins of the fourteenth-century moated Scotney Castle.

Fourteenth-century moated Scotney Castle, set in woods and parkland, is situated a short distance south of Tunbridge Wells. Among all its native and exotic trees perhaps the most interesting and possibly the oldest on the estate is an ancient hornbeam, which stands on the edge of a wood a few hundred metres south of the castle.

Hornbeams (*Carpinus betulus*) are slightly smaller than many of the other native deciduous forest trees. They have grey fluted trunks and ovate leaves (6 to 8 centimetres long) that are similar to those of beech trees (*Fagus sylvatica*), but with serrated edges and distinctive deep ribs following the lateral veins. They have been sought after for their timber, fuel wood and fodder for thousands of years (see also Hatfield Forest, p. 84). More recently the timber has been used in the production of drumsticks, piano hammers and snooker cues. The trees also have the ability to grow into durable and dense hedges.

As is traditional with hornbeams, the tree at Scotney has been pollarded for around 600 years, and displays the associated features of a broad trunk and reduced height, as well as the development of aerial roots in the cavity of its hollow trunk (see also Introduction, p. 10). After they have reabsorbed the nutrients that have been newly released by fungal decay, the old aerial roots take on a new role: they act as a natural brace that holds together the hollow shell of the tree's trunk providing additional strength, which is what has happened with the hornbeam at Scotney. Pollarding was carried out in Kent until Victorian times when there was still a demand for vast quantities of small-gauge timber, particularly for use in charcoal-making and for firewood in the City of London. The hornbeam pollards were vital in providing London with bread, as the wood was ideal for quickly heating up the ovens prior to the advent of electricity.

The wonderful limb-like aerial root that has formed in the hollow trunk of an ancient hornbeam pollard (*Carpinus betulus*) in order to take advantage of the nutrients being released as the trunk decays.

A 600-year-old hornbeam (*Carpinus betulus*) continues to leaf and fruit despite its advanced age because it has been regularly pollarded over many years.

Stourhead
Wiltshire

The landscaped garden at Stourhead is the centrepiece of the 1,070-hectare estate that lies close to the town of Mere. It is the result of the vision of Henry Hoare II, who created the major features between 1741 and 1780. His idea was to establish a garden surrounding a lake, similar in style to that at Stowe in Buckinghamshire, with views inspired by scenes from Italian art. After Henry Hoare's death, work on the garden was continued by his grandson, Richard Colt Hoare, who was responsible for adding many of the fine broadleaved trees, especially maple (*Acers*), horse chestnut (*Aesculus hippocastanum*), plane (*Platanus*) and tulip (*Liriodendron tulipifera*) trees. Beyond the ornamental gardens there are areas of parkland and woodland that are home to ancient native trees, including oak (*Quercus*), beech (*Fagus sylvatica*), ash (*Fraxinus excelsior*) and sweet chestnut (*Castanea sativa*).

Set within the ornamental gardens that surround the main lake is one of the finest collections of exotic trees and shrubs in Britain, with many being among the earliest recorded introductions to the country. In spring the trees are festooned with blossom or feature large scented flowers, including azalea (*Azalea*), rhododendron (*Rhododendron*) and oriental cherries (*Acer*). Stourhead is famous for its autumn colours: a spectacular combination of native trees such as beech, oak and ash interspersed with more exotic specimens such as cherries, maples and North American oaks.

Grand redwoods

Many of the introduced trees have thrived over the last 200 years, including the collection of redwoods. There are grand examples of all three types of redwood: the coast redwood

A view across the lake at Stourhead, which is encircled by an arboretum of native and exotic tree species.

Stourton Castle, by Peter Richard Hoare (1772–1849).

(*Sequoia sempervirens*), the giant redwood (*Sequoiadendron giganteum*) and the dawn redwood (*Metasequoia glyptostroboides*). The dawn redwood displays the characteristic tapering trunk and feathery needles that are reminiscent of the swamp cypresses (*Taxodium sp.*), which can also be found close to the lake edge. Both of these conifers are deciduous, in that they lose their needles every autumn. For many years the dawn redwood was thought to have been extinct until plant explorer Ernest Wilson discovered a few isolated individuals on his travels through China. Today the largest coast redwood in the garden has a girth of 7.22 metres and that of the greatest giant redwood is 7.02 metres. While these are vast by British standards, they are mere saplings when compared to the biggest trees in their native California, which have girths of 22.7 metres and 24 metres respectively.

A touch of the exotic

Stourhead has one of the largest tulip trees in England, which can be found close to the ornamental bridge on the south side of the lake. Tulip trees are relatively fast growing and at around 200 years old this example already has a girth of 6.55 metres. They are deciduous and are members of the magnolia family, and this particular species is native to North America. Their name is derived from the tulip-like green and yellow flowers that appear in early summer. In the wild the trees can grow to heights of over 50 metres.

Many of the exotic trees at Stourhead are what are known as 'champion trees', which means they are the largest of their type either locally or nationally. At the time of going to press, Stourhead is the home to Britain's champion English oak tree (*Quercus robur*). In 2014 specialist aboriculturalists climbed to the top of one of the trees in a group of very lofty old oaks set in deciduous woodland that wraps around the western side of the main garden. They established that it was the tallest English oak in the country with a height of 40.4 metres. It is apt for the National Trust, whose emblem is an English oak leaf, to be the custodian of this remarkable specimen.

The mystery of the sweet chestnut avenues

Stourhead, like many of the great houses in Britain, has a fine collection of sweet chestnuts (*Castanea sativa*). They were a particular favourite of landscape designers such as Capability Brown and Humphry Repton, who either planted new trees or left mature ones standing as significant features of the landscapes they were creating. No doubt sweet chestnuts appeared in the original plans of both Henry Hoare II and Richard Colt Hoare.

It is thought that sweet chestnuts were introduced by the Romans into Britain after which they became naturalised. They are striking trees when mature, with their chocolate

One of the largest tulip trees (*Liriodendron tulipifera*) in Britain stands on the water's edge on the south side of the main lake.

The larger and more ancient sweet chestnut trees (*Castanea sativa*) in the avenue lead to the former location of the main house.

brown, deeply fissured bark sometimes forming herringbone patterns and great spreading crowns of glossy green foliage. For this reason they have been used widely in the historic parks and gardens in Britain. In the seventeenth century the fashion of creating long sweeping, formal avenues of trees on the approaches to grand houses became established, a trend imported from France.

On the route from the road to the main house at Stourhead there is a curving avenue of sweet chestnut trees that leads towards the eastern face of the striking white mansion. They are in a straight line heading almost due north. Although they still mark the beginning of the present-day avenue that runs up to the main house, the trees that sweep off in the direction of the mansion are noticeably younger and smaller. By studying historic maps the reason for this becomes apparent. The large ancient sweet chestnut avenue once led to the original property of the Barons of Stourton, who had lived at the Stourhead estate for 500 years before the Hoare family bought it in 1717. Old Stourton House stood upon a site immediately in front of the present mansion and the road leading to Maiden Bradley. The site can be recognised by the undulating ground and a few old sweet chestnut trees. Henry Hoare II demolished the property around 1721 before beginning the construction of the current Palladian-style house.

The sweet chestnut trees (*Castanea sativa*) in the curving avenue leading towards the main house today are noticeably younger and smaller than those in the original avenue.

Opposite: Within the ornamental garden is a large and fine example of a dawn redwood (*Metasequoia glyptostroboides*) from China, which was once thought to be extinct.

Stowe
Buckinghamshire

Stowe was acquired in 1985 by the National Trust and today comprises 300 hectares of historic landscaped gardens with follies, lakes and magnificent avenues of trees.

The main landscaping of the estate started in 1711 when garden designer extraordinaire Charles Bridgeman began creating the gardens that we see today.[1] Bridgeman took landscapes out of the traditional mould of straight geometric patterns and introduced a more naturalistic approach, the precursor to Capability Brown. He was succeeded by William Kent, who was in turn followed by Capability Brown in 1841. Stowe has a staggering 17 avenues, two of which are stylish entrances that feature lime (*Tilia*): the Grand Avenue and the Oxford Avenue, planted in the 1770s and 1790s respectively.

At the heart of the estate are two lakes fringed by heavily landscaped grounds with numerous extraordinary statues and follies. John Michael Rysbrack, the famous eighteenth-century sculptor, carved the Saxon Deities and eight of the British Worthies. The design was laid out as a series of 'pictures' as opposed to sweeping panoramic vistas depicting scenes from antiquity. The Elysian Fields allude to 'Elysium' in Greek mythology, which was a concept of the afterlife where worthy mortals chosen by the gods resided: 'The Elysian Fields or Elysium refer to a beautiful meadow in Homer where the favoured of Zeus enjoy perfect happiness.'[2]

The Elysian Fields surround two narrow lakes, which are known as the river Styx after the river in Greek mythology that formed the boundary between earth and the underworld. Along the lakeside are many exotic trees and shrubs that were planted by Bridgeman in the early eighteenth century. Among them is an extraordinary yew (*Taxus baccata*). It is known as a 'phoenix', or 'walking', yew because where its branches have dipped down and touched the ground new trees have taken root: rising from the humus rather than from the ashes, as in mythology.

Dead beautiful

Just beyond the southern edge of the formal gardens are the remains of a huge ash tree (*Fraxinus excelsior*). It is just a shell now but reminds us just how valuable ancient trees can be; the tree may be dead but it is full of life. On the inside, a stem

Opposite and right: A young elder (*Sambucus nigra*) growing out through the shell of a large deceased ash (*Fraxinus excelsior*) is taking advantage of the rich compost in the decaying trunk.

A 'phoenix' or 'walking' yew (*Taxus baccata*) on the edge of the Elysian Fields looks like a writhing serpent that is moving at glacial speed.

of an elder (*Sambucus nigra*) can be seen wriggling towards the light. It has taken advantage of the rich humus that has collected within the hollow trunk.

Dead trees and fallen branches continue to contribute to local ecosystems for tens or hundreds of years, providing a rich array of microhabitats for a whole range of saproxylic organisms such as fungi and specialist invertebrates, as well as mosses, bats and birds, some of which have a very specific relationship with the dead tree. There are 2,023 different invertebrate species in Britain that are dependent on decaying wood in order to complete their life cycles. This represents about 7 per cent of our entire invertebrate fauna.

The Farey Oak

Just beyond the south-west wall of the formal garden is a spectacular oak (*Quercus*) known as the 'Farey Oak'. It takes its name from the former owner of the field in which it stands. It is a rather squat ancient oak with a girth of 7.14 metres, and may be over 600 hundred years old. What is remarkable about the tree is not so much its age but what it represents. More than a thousand years ago large ancient and distinctive trees were often used to mark boundaries or the centres of village communities. They were powerful symbols of identity especially in a landscape devoid of other distinguishing features. In the Domesday book the sub-division of a shire or county was known as a 'hundred'. The focal point of many of these 'hundreds' was an ancient or large tree and this was often reflected in the name, such as Becontree in Essex or Appletree in Derbyshire.

The Farey Oak was known to have stood in the hamlet of Lamport, beside the Rattly Road that runs between New Inn and Towcester. The road and town have disappeared but New Inn still exists and houses the National Trust's visitor centre for Stowe.

1. Clarke 1985, pp. 72–83.
2. Bloom (ed.) 2001, p. 63.

The Farey Oak (*Quercus*) marked the central point of a busy village more than 500 years ago. Today only the tree remains.

Tolpuddle Martyrs' Tree
Dorset

Every weekend in July the population of the tiny hamlet of Tolpuddle swells by several thousand people. Great crowds gather to listen to the political speeches by Labour politicians and Union leaders. The event marks the birth of the British Trade Union movement, the focal point of which is the old sycamore tree that stands on the village green. It was here in 1833 that six men, known as the Tolpuddle Martyrs, first met to form the 'Friendly Society of Agricultural Workers'.

Detail of the Tolpuddle Martyrs' commemorative plaque on the Magistrates' Court building.

It is not surprising that they gathered beneath a prominent tree, as such specimens, sometimes known as 'trysting' trees, have been favoured as meeting places for centuries around the world.

The Tolpuddle Martyrs' tree is an ancient sycamore (*Acer pseudoplatinus*) that has been reliably aged to over 300 years old. It has a huge, hollow trunk, which, without the care and management of the National Trust, would almost certainly have collapsed by now. The installation of several iron cross members on the inside of the hollow may have helped stop the tree from falling apart. The fact that it has continued to be pollarded has also greatly increased its chances of surviving long into the future, perhaps for another 300 years.

The 'martyrs' were complaining about the Enclosure Acts, which led to many local people losing the right to work on communal land and instead having to work for wages from the new landowners. The power wielded by the landowners became excessive and desperate workers were faced with a choice of working for a mere nine shillings a week or leaving their village to seek work in the cities. They grouped together and petitioned the local landowner, James Frampton, for a fair wage. The plan backfired and the six were arrested for 'administering unlawful oaths'. They were transported to Australia in 1834 to work on the chain gangs.

Working people in Britain were so incensed at the harsh sentences that very soon over a quarter of a million had signed a petition for the sentences to be commuted. When a procession of more than 30,000 people marched down Whitehall, in London, in support of the Tolpuddle Six, the government was forced to free them; they returned as martyrs.

The 300-year-old Tolpuddle Martyrs' sycamore (*Acer pseudoplatinus*) in winter, with its huge trunk and small branches that are the result of regular pollarding.

The Enclosure Acts

In 1801, Parliament passed the General Enclosure Act, by which any village, where three-quarters of the landowners agreed, could enclose its common land. This had a devastating effect on the rural population many of whom were forced to leave their homes and seek employment in the towns and cities. Ancient trees and woodland were cleared to make way for the larger arable fields created by enclosure.

John Clare wrote about the inequity of the enclosures as can be seen in the second half of his poem, 'The Mores':

> Free as spring clouds and wild as summer flowers
> is faded all – a hope that blossomed free,
> And hath been once, no more shall ever be
> Inclosure came and trampled on the grave
> Of labour's rights and left the poor a slave
> And memory's pride ere want to wealth did bow
> is both the shadow and the substance now
> The sheep and cows were free to range as then
> Where change might prompt nor felt the bonds of men
> Cows went and came, with evening morn and night,
> To the wild pasture as their common right
> And sheep, unfolded with the rising sun
> Heard the swains shout and felt their freedom won
> Tracked the red fallow field and heath and plain
> Then met the brook and drank and roamed again
> The brook that dribbled on as clear as glass
> Beneath the roots they hid among the grass
> While the glad shepherd traced their tracks along
> Free as the lark and happy as her song
> But now all's fled and flats of many a dye
> That seemed to lengthen with the following eye
> Moors, loosing from the sight, far, smooth, and blea
> Where swopt the plover in its pleasure free
> Are vanished now with commons wild and gay
> As poet's visions of life's early day
> Mulberry-bushes where the boy would run
> To fill his hands with fruit are grubbed and done.[1]

1. Robinson and Summerfield (eds) 1966, p. 169.

Ullswater
Cumbria

At the western end of Ullswater Lake in the Cumbrian fells lie several properties belonging to the National Trust, including Gowbarrow Park, Glencoyne Farm and Glenamara Park. Each of these have examples of historic 'wood pasture' typical to the Lake District.

Wood pasture consists of large open-grown trees, such as oak (*Quercus*), ash (*Fraxinus*), alder (*Alnus*) and birch (*Betula*), set in grazed grassland or heathland. In the Lake District this system is not only confined to the lowland areas but can also be seen at relatively high altitudes, such as at Gowbarrow Park. Open-grown trees in wood pasture live to greater ages than in the competitive environment of an ancient wood. Around the shores of Ullswater the ancient trees in the wood pasture provide habitats for a number of rare and endangered species: fungi such as the big blue pinkgill (*Entoloma bloxamii*), pink waxcap *(Hygrocybe calyptriformis)* and the date-coloured waxcap (*Hygrocybe spadicea*); birds including the lesser spotted woodpecker (*Dendrocopos minor*),

The Sitka spruce (*Picea sitchensis*) at Aira Force is one of the largest in Britain and has a curiously upturned branch that makes it look like Pinocchio's long-nosed face.

Ancient wood pasture on the edge of Ullswater, a scene that is thought to have changed little over the last 5,000 years.

An ancient wood pasture alder (*Alnus*) on the high slopes of Gowbarrow Fell.

spotted fly catcher (*Muscicapa striata*) and wood warbler (*Phylloscopus sibilatrix*); and bats, notably the Natterer's bat (*Myotis nattereri*) and the noctule bat (*Nyctalus noctula*).

The shape of the open-grown trees is different to that of woodland trees. The trunks are generally shorter, the canopies take the form of a wide-spreading dome for the optimum capture of sunlight and they usually have a system of substantial buttress roots in response to being more exposed to gales. Individual ancient trees can form ecosystems in their own right with an oak able to provide niches for more species than any other British tree. A single open-grown oak can support over 300 varieties of lichen and nearly the same number of insect species.

Research by the ecologist Franz Vera has pointed to the fact that, rather than Europe being covered in an extensive wildwood as was once believed, the ancient landscape was similar to savanna.[1] He studied dung beetle fossils to show that the primeval forest was more likely to have been a mosaic of woodland and grassland punctuated by many large open-grown trees.

Aira Force waterfall

The name Aira Force is from the O/N *eyrara* – meaning 'gravel-bank stream or river' – and O/N *fors* – meaning 'waterfall'. In contrast to the ancient managed treescape around Ullswater is the arboretum at the base of the waterfall,

On Gowbarrow Fell, an ancient ash pollard (*Fraxinus excelsior*) is covered in a variety of rare lichens.

Cumbria is one of the few locations in England and Wales where the pollution-sensitive lichen, tree lungwort (*Lobaria pulmonaria*), can grow.

which forms part of the 300-hectare Gowbarrow Park, created in 1846 by the Howard family of Greystoke Castle, Penrith. The arboretum was acquired by the National Trust in 1906 and includes more than 200 conifers. Some are among the tallest trees in Cumbria, including a fine Sitka spruce (*Picea sitchensis*) over 35 metres in height. One of its branches is reminiscent of Pinocchio's long-nosed face.

Lichens

Beautiful pale green lichens can be seen on large trees close to Aira Force and in the wood pasture of Glencoyne Farm and Gowbarrow Fell. Prior to the Industrial Revolution it is likely that there would have been abundant populations of lichens growing throughout Britain. However, species such as *Lobaria* are particularly susceptible to sulphur dioxide pollution, produced from coal-fire smoke and which falls as 'acid rain'. Today *Lobaria virens* and *L. pulmonaria* are found only in parts of the New Forest and the south-west of England, and two areas of Cumbria.

A noctule bat (*Nyctalua noctula*).

The preferred habitat of *Lobaria* is the acidic bark of broad-leaved trees, especially oak, ash, sycamore (*Acer pseudoplatanus*), hazel (*Corylus*), elm (*Ulmus*) and beech (*Fagus*). Even in the relatively clean air of Cumbria *Lobaria* are declining and it is thought that nitrous oxides from vehicle exhaust fumes might be one of the reasons for this. The major episode of lichen damage in the recent past was caused by Dutch elm disease and currently it is thought that ash dieback (*Hymenoscyphus fraxineus*) will lead to the disappearance of millions of ashes and with them their associated lichen flora.

1. Vera 2000.

Vyne Estate
Hampshire

Just north of Basingstoke lies the Vyne Estate, set in 450 hectares of countryside. The centrepiece is the sixteenth-century country house with its 16-hectare ornamental garden, built for Lord Sandys, King Henry VIII's Lord Chamberlain. The extensive parkland that surrounds the house and gardens has a fine collection of ancient trees that dates back to the medieval deer park of around 1268.

While the great storms of 1987 and 1991 removed a number of ancient trees from the landscape many have survived and can still be seen today. With its fascinating heritage, it is not surprising that very old trees are scattered across the estate, including ancient hornbeam pollards (*Carpinus betulus*), parkland oaks (*Quercus*) and wetland species such as willow (*Salix*) and alder (*Alnus*). During the 1880s, owner Chaloner Chute instigated a tree-planting programme that included the avenue of limes (*Tilia*) running northwards from the garden house to the walled garden.

The north front of the house seen across the lake.

The Hundred Guinea Oak

The most famous, and in many ways the most magnificent, tree in the grounds is the 'Hundred Guinea Oak', which stands close to the road on the south-east side of the ornamental garden next to what is possibly the earliest domed garden building in England, dating from around 1635 and designed by John Webb. The Hundred Guinea Oak is believed to have gained its name when William John Chute was offered £100 for the tree by a passing naval agent seeking timber for vessels around the time of Trafalgar. Chute, who was well known for not running the estate on an economic basis – refusing to modernise farming practices or sell any trees during his tenure – turned the agent down. It is said that the same agent returned shortly afterwards with a revised offer of 100 guineas, and Chute responded that 'any tree that increases in value by 5 per cent overnight is too valuable an investment to lose'.[1] The story has elements of truth about it as it was common at the time for the Navy to seek out trees that had limbs growing at particular angles or in specific combinations, which could be easily fashioned into bulkheads and other structural components for use in ships. Furthermore the same story is recorded in the handwritten diaries of William Lyde Wiggett Chute in the nineteenth century.

The Hundred Guinea Oak is a spectacular tree: it is 22 metres tall with a girth of exactly 8 metres at a height of 1.5 metres from the ground. It is considered to be over 600 years old and therefore significantly pre-dates the buildings and ornamental gardens around it. One of its most unusual features is that it leans at an angle of 40 degrees to the south-east. The canopy has been gradually reduced over the last few years and there is now a plan to construct a metal half-ring

The ancient Hundred Guinea Oak (*Quercus petraea*) leans at a steep angle and has developed extra buttresses to take the strain.

An ancient hornbeam pollard (*Carpinus betulus*) stands in wood pasture at the Vyne Estate that has remained largely unchanged for over 1,000 years.

The Hundred Guinea Oak (*Quercus petraea*) has a girth of 8 metres and would have been identified as a tree potentially useful for the Royal Navy.

attached to supports in order to catch the tree if its roots fail, so preventing it from falling onto the public road. It has responded to the great strain of holding itself up at such an acute angle by producing an enormous supporting buttress opposite to the direction in which it is leaning.

Oak and shipbuilding

Britain relied on its war fleet for defence from the Middle Ages to the mid-nineteenth century and its ships were predominantly made from oak. Henry VIII is credited with establishing the Royal Navy and by the time of his death in 1547 Britain already had a fleet of 40 warships.

By the beginning of the seventeenth century oaks were so important to Britain's national security that a survey was undertaken in 1608 to establish how many were actually suitable for shipbuilding. The results showed that 123,927 oaks had the necessary trunk and branch shapes for a ship's construction. A further survey in 1708 revealed that the number of oaks useful to the Navy had fallen to just 12,476.[2]

The main areas from which oaks were harvested were the New Forest (Hampshire), Alice Holt (Surrey) and the Brecon Beacons (Powys, South Wales), as well as the many private estates in the south of England such as the Vyne Estate, which were relatively close to the main ship-building docks of Portsmouth, Southampton and Plymouth.

A 3D laser scan of the entire structure of Nelson's HMS *Victory* in 2013 revealed that it was made using timber from around 6,000 trees of which 90 per cent were oak. The laser takes 500,000 measurements per second, and each scan lasts 3.5 minutes. In total there are almost 90 billion measurements in the new model, all accurate to within 1 mm.[3]

1. Chute 2005, p. 43.
2. *Journal of the House of Commons*, vol. 44 (1708), p. 563.
3. The National Royal Navy Museum, 15 July 2013, hmsvictory.com, accessed January 2016.

Wakehurst Place

West Sussex

A recently pruned ancient yew (*Taxus baccata*) close to the main house has a sculptural beauty.

Wakehurst Place, owned by the National Trust, is managed by the Royal Botanic Gardens, Kew. The estate was bought by Gerald Loder, a former President of the Royal Horticultural Society, in 1903. He developed the gardens and established many of the present plant collections, particularly those from eastern Asia and the southern continents. Wakehurst Place is also home to the Millennium Seed Bank, which opened in 2000 and currently holds the largest and most diverse collection of wild species in the world.

The estate has superb examples of redwoods (*Sequoia*) from USA, southern beech (*Nothofagus*) from Chile and acers from Japan, as well as native British trees.

A number of yew trees (*Taxus baccata*) were recently examined by dendrochronologist Dr Andy Moir. He took tiny core samples from six trees that enabled the rings to be counted while causing only minimal damage. The smaller diameter younger trees provided entire tree ring sequences allowing their ages to be accurately estimated to the very year they germinated. However, the larger diameter trees, as is the case with all ancient yews, had already begun to go hollow and so only partial ring sequences were available. Comparing the partial tree ring data with the known growth rates of younger trees in similar conditions, the largest of the yew trees, with a girth of 6.04 metres, was found to be around 620 years old.

The discovery that there were yew trees planted in the gardens more than 600 years ago helped former Head Gardener, Andy Jackson, prove what he had long suspected: that there had been a fourteenth-century house on the site before the current Elizabethan mansion was constructed.

A prominent ancient yew stands on the lawn in front of the main house. Over the years the tree had rapidly declined, so it has been heavily pruned to reinvigorate it and to encourage it to send out new growth from the stem. With a girth of 4.52 metres, it is believed to have germinated around 1650. The pruning has revealed a large fluted trunk that is especially beautiful when viewed on a wet day when the strong pink, purple, turquoise and chestnut colouring is most noticeable.

Remarkable roots

To the north of the grounds in an area known as Rock Walk is a group of equally remarkable yew trees. Their size indicates that they were probably planted in Victorian times. What is striking about this group of yews is the way their roots have spread down through the large sandstone boulders on which they perch. They have developed extensive root systems much as they would have done had they been growing in places such as the high exposed rock faces of the Lake District or the Yorkshire Dales. Some yew trees growing in stressed conditions on cliff faces form miniature trunks only a few centimetres in diameter yet can be hundreds of years old.

Yew trees (*Taxus baccata*) planted on the sandstone boulders along Rock Walk display their remarkable tenacious twisting roots.

Woolsthorpe Manor

Lincolnshire

Sir Isaac Newton was born on Christmas day 1642 at Woolsthorpe Manor, a remarkably fine late seventeenth-century yeoman farmer's house in rural Lincolnshire. As well as being the birthplace of such a great scientist and mathematician, it is the home to possibly the most important and historic tree in the scientific world: the 'Newton Apple Tree'. In addition to its association with Newton, it is also believed to be the oldest verifiable apple tree on the planet, with an age in excess of 350 years. It was while sitting under this very tree in the garden at Woolsthorpe in late summer 1666 that Newton observed an apple fall. This unremarkable event stimulated a train of thought that was to go on and revolutionise the understanding of our universe and effectively facilitate space travel a few hundred years later. His close friend William Stuckley wrote:

> The notion of gravitation ... was occassion'd by the fall of an apple, as he [Newton] sat in contemplative mood. Why should that apple always descend perpendicularly to the ground, thought he to himself, why not go sideways or upwards, but constantly to the Earth's centre, Assuredly, the Earth draws it ... there is a power, like that we here call gravity, which extends itself thro' the universe.[1]

The story of the falling apple was thought to have been a myth but Newton was known to have given accounts to a number of friends and acquaintances, including writer and philosopher Voltaire and John Conduitt, Newton's assistant at the Royal Mint. It was Conduitt who first wrote down the story in 1726, the year before Newton's death.[2]

At the time of Newton's discovery there was just a single apple tree in the garden at Woolsthorpe Manor, a variety known as the 'Flower of Kent'. In 1820 the Revd Charles Turner made a sketch of the tree and house, which clearly shows the position and shape of the standing tree along with one of the main stems lying on the ground after a storm in 1816. Rather than being felled after being damaged, the tree was allowed to continue to live to such a phenomenal age in recognition of the connection with Newton.

Fruit trees are not renowned for their longevity and in normal circumstances an apple tree would not survive much beyond 100 years. At 350 years, Newton's Apple Tree appears to still be in good health but in order to preserve its lineage a number of cuttings have been taken and grafted onto root stock to create the small orchard that now surrounds it. Interestingly, each tree produces subtly different fruit because of the variation in root stock.

The apples on the Newton Apple Tree (*Malus pumila var.*) have distinctive red and yellow banding, although each time it is grafted onto a new root stock the apples display a different pattern.

Newton's Apple Tree (*Malus pumila var.*) in full leaf. It is the oldest verifiable apple tree in the world.

The cultural significance of apples

Apple trees are part of the genus *Malus* comprising around 25 species of small deciduous trees that have a wide distribution throughout the northern hemisphere. The orchard apple (*Malus domestica*) is distinct from the wild crab apple (*Malus sylvestris*), as it originated from the wild Asian apple (*Malus sieversii*) and over centuries of cultivation and selection has developed into the 7,500 varieties worldwide with considerably larger and sweeter fruit. When a domestic apple tree reverts to its wild form it produces small, bitter fruit once more and regains the thorns of its wild relatives: the genus *Malus* is part of the *Roscaceae* family.

Unsurprisingly, with all their well-known health benefits apples have had a long and varied cultural and mythological history. They are particularly associated with love, fertility and marriage and feature in many European fairy tales from the Middle Ages. Apples were used in stories to win the affection of a loved one and in real life they were presented to pregnant women to help guarantee healthy offspring.

1. Stukeley 1752.
2. See Hall 1999, p. 13 onwards.

Newton's Apple Tree as it was in 1840, from William Stukeley, *Memoirs of Sir Isaac Newton's Life*, 1752.

The Future

We have come a very long way in the past 20 to 30 years in the understanding of the physiology of ancient trees, their needs, the tangible threats they are under and what we can do to allow them to adapt and adjust to their modern environment. Thirty years ago it was not given much thought. The old trees, though loved and admired by some, were mostly ignored by individuals and organisations, including the National Trust. Britain was unaware of just how significant such trees were within a European context. We now think that there might be more ancient trees in Britain than in all the rest of northern Europe put together and the Trust has a larger number on its properties than any other landowner. This demonstrates just how important the Trust's trees are and why it is vital that they are managed to the highest standards.

Armed with an inventory of all the Trust's ancient and veteran trees, where they are at greatest risk and how best to look after them, the organisation is in a fantastic position to lead the way in their management and to act as an example to others. The future threats of pests and diseases may well demonstrate the significance of many ancient trees. It is not purely luck that has enabled some trees to live upwards of a thousand years when the vast majority of their species die before they have reached half or a quarter of that age. These individuals may contain genes, or endophytes, fungi or bacteria, which have protected them from pathogens throughout their lives.

Wooden stairs to the first floor from the atrium at Heelis, the Central Office of the National Trust, designed by architects Feilden Clegg Bradley and containing timber grown in the Trust's own woods.

Ensuring that there is no further avoidable loss of any of its ancient trees is a massive challenge for the Trust, requiring generations of dedicated and highly skilled staff carrying out sensitive husbandry around all such specimens. Each tree should ideally have a management plan, detailing what work should be undertaken on and around it, and on what cycle.

Lapsed pollard trees that have been brought back into cycle require re-pollarding at a schedule according to the species and its vulnerability. Pollards that have not been recently managed need their crowns carefully and slowly reduced, sometimes over decades, to bring them down to a height where their trunks and root systems are able to support their crowns without risk of collapse or wind damage.

Trees within the historic wood pastures need to be free from encroachment by vigorous naturally regenerated trees; this requires repeated scrub clearance and tree felling followed by grazing to prevent competition. During the clearance phase suitable replacement trees can be identified and retained as future ancient trees. If the wood pasture has a significant age imbalance, then it may be necessary to veteranise some of these trees to stimulate mature features at a much younger age. This helps to create habitat continuity, which is vital for many of the rare specialist flora and fauna associated with very old trees.

In all habitats where ancient trees are found it is important that there are replacement trees of varying ages, from young saplings through to ancient specimens, to ensure continuity of habitat for their associated specialist species. What is crucial is that this is done over centuries and never stops.

One of the great ancient beech pollards (*Fagus sylvatica*) in Frithsden Woods at the Ashridge Estate displaying fruiting fungal bodies and decaying wood, which provide habitats for a wide variety of saproxylic invertebrates.

All too often in the past parklands have had comprehensive management plans identifying the historic loss of trees, which then stimulate rapid planting over a short time creating another age imbalance. We need to think long term; we need to think in tree time.

As this book goes to print Europe's ash trees (*Fraxinus*) are being destroyed by *Hymenoscyphus fraxineus* (previously called *Chalara fraxinea*), which causes ash dieback. This newly identified pathogen was first described in 2006 in Poland, has now spread across most of northern Europe and was recorded in a nursery in the UK in 2012. It is infecting more than 90 per cent of ash trees in some countries leading to a significant number of tree deaths. Ancient ash trees may well prove to be resistant to ash dieback; time will tell. National Trust staff have already collected seed from its oldest ash trees for the Millennium Seed Bank in case they should prove vital in the long-term survival of the species.

We are all now more aware of the incredible importance of these irreplaceable old trees and have a better understanding of their requirements, their physiology and their complex symbiotic relationships with mycorrhizal and wood-decaying fungi. Therefore, these crown jewels of our natural world should have a secure future to inspire and enthral forthcoming generations.

Glossary

Aerial roots – Roots that grow above the ground. Ancient trees have stored valuable nutrients within their non-living heartwood for hundreds of years. Initially this was essential to provide strength, rigidity and weight to keep the tree upright and intact. As the trunk grows larger and the crown reduces in size, the tree no longer requires this massive volume of wood to help support itself. Wood decaying endophytic fungi (see **Endophytes**) are stimulated by conditions within the tree's heartwood to begin decaying the wood. Eventually the tree starts to grow aerial roots from its inner living wood into the recently decayed heartwood, reabsorbing the previously unobtainable nutrients. Over many decades this decay process progresses and produces a tree with a hollow trunk. The old aerial roots can then form an internal bracing, helping to support the tree's fragile shell.

Ancient tree – A tree considerably older than most others of its species: for example, for birch or apple it would be 200 years, for beech 300 years, for oak or sweet chestnut 600 years and for yew a staggering 800 years.

Ancient Tree Forum – A small charity whose mission is to champion ancient trees and thereby safeguard their biological, cultural and heritage value, now and in the future, for the whole of society.

Arboretum – A collection of different tree and shrub species created for scientific, educational and/or ornamental purposes.

Aril – An additional, usually fleshy, seed casing, such as the berry-like covering on yew seeds; produced by various kinds of plant to entice birds or mammals to eat the seeds and thereby distribute them.

Canopy – The entire roof-like spread of the leaves and branches of a group of trees or a single tree. In low-density woodland, there may be gaps in the canopy but in a closed-canopy woodland there are no gaps through which new trees may emerge.

Coppicing – A traditional woodland management system whereby broadleaved trees or shrubs are cut at ground level to encourage re-growth and are re-cut on a rotation the length of which depends on the species and desired material. Hazel is still cut on a short cycle of seven to ten years to provide material for hurdles and thatching, whereas oak was historically cut less frequently (every 25 to 30 years) to provide bark for tanning, firewood, charcoal and building material.

Copse – A small group of trees also referred to as a spinney, grove or thicket.

Ecosystem – A biological interconnected community of organisms including plants, animals and fungi that interact with aspects of the physical environment, such as air, minerals and water.

Enclosure Acts – A series of Acts of Parliament dating mainly from the 1750s by which open fields and common land were enclosed. This created property rights for individuals over land that had been considered common land with shared commoners' rights. There were over 5,200 Enclosure Acts, which enclosed a fifth of the area of England.

Endophytes – Organisms, often fungi or bacteria, which live between the cells of their host. The relationship varies; it can be mutually beneficial but can sometimes become harmful. Some fungi are thought to help protect their host from damaging pathogens.

Epiphytes – Plants that live on other plants. The name derives from the Greek *epi* – meaning 'upon' – and *phyton* – meaning 'plant'.

Estover – One of several commoners' rights dating back to medieval times, from the French *estovoir* meaning 'that which is necessary'. It conveys the right to take limbs from trees for repairs to buildings or to make necessary tools and implements, all essential for the commoners' survival.

Exotic trees – In Great Britain, tree species that have not been naturally present since the last Ice Age. Seeds from such trees have been transported by humans, including the Romans and, more recently, the great plant collectors of the eighteenth and nineteenth centuries, who introduced countless ornamental and commercial species.

Faggots – Bundles of small branches tied together, usually collected as fuel for fires.

Forest – Although the modern meaning of the word is synonymous with woodland, that is, land covered in dense trees, the medieval meaning was an area set aside for the purpose of hunting noble game, such as roe deer, fallow deer and boar, and restricted to royalty. In England, the concept was introduced by the Normans and for several centuries vast expanses of the country were reserved for the monarch or, by his permission, the aristocracy. A medieval forest was largely open meadows containing individual scattered trees with a mosaic of copses, woods and scrub. This allowed the king and his retinue to gallop at full pace in pursuit of game.

Functional units – A tree has a vascular network for the transport of water and dissolved nutrients. These flow mostly upwards or downwards but they can also flow laterally. Thus, for example, water absorbed by a root on one side of the tree could be transported to leaves on the opposite side of the crown. Lateral flow can occur freely in a young tree, since its vascular network acts as a single interconnected entity. As a tree ages, however, it tends to become increasingly divided into a number of functional units. Each of these includes a discrete part of the crown of the tree, which is connected via a sector of the trunk to a specific section of the root system. By dividing into functional units, the tree is more likely to survive in the long term. If one unit becomes damaged in some way, this does not necessarily affect the other units. This is one of many strategies that trees have developed to allow them to live for remarkably long periods.

Girth – The measured circumference of a tree at a set height, usually 1.5 metres above the ground. Measuring the girth is the only way we can estimate the age of ancient trees in the field, since virtually all are hollow, making it impossible to extract a complete core of annual rings for counting. Research by John White of the Forestry Commission and others on various tree species has shown that the girth of most trees increases fairly consistently in similar growing conditions: more quickly in early life, then at a reasonably steady rate for a very long period. Girth-to-age tables have been produced for many of the most common British species giving an estimated age for trees at different girths. This forms the basis of our ageing of old trees but it becomes difficult in ancient trees, which may be growing much more slowly than indicated in the tables. These tables are continually being modified and adjusted for local conditions.

Heartwood – When wood first forms under the bark of a tree, it is a living tissue that conducts water and mineral nutrients from the roots to the leaves. This is sapwood, which also stores carbohydrates. After a certain number of years, which varies depending both on species and individuals, the tree's oldest and innermost annual ring of sapwood becomes inert, no longer functioning as part of the vascular network. This happens in successive rings of old sapwood for the rest of the tree's life, while new annual rings of sapwood continue to form under the bark. Thus, as the tree gets older, the proportion of non-conductive wood increases, eventually comprising the bulk of the tree's trunk. In many species, it takes no more than a year or two for each successive ring of oldest sapwood to become non-conductive. In these species, the older central wood forms a distinct heartwood. Also, in some species, this contains natural preservatives, which slow down decay.

Hectare – A metric unit of area that is 10,000 square metres, or roughly 2.47 acres, or 100 metres by 100 metres.

Hyphae – The very fine hair-like threads that make up the body (known as a mycelium) of a fungus. The hyphae absorb nutrients and water.

Layering – For many species of broadleaf tree, when a lower limb succumbs to the forces of gravity and rests on the ground it has the ability to grow roots from the point of contact. Meanwhile, new stems or branches grow from the same point. Over time the new root system provides the stems or branches with enough nutrients to become self-sufficient. The connecting limb becomes redundant and may eventually die and decay, leaving little evidence to the untrained eye that the tree is actually a clone of the mother tree. A similar process can happen when a tree falls over but still retains some functioning root system. Roots can develop on the underside of the tree's trunk directly beneath branches. Over many years these limbs can form a straight line of new trees; again, after some time the original tree trunk may decay and disappear leaving a curious short avenue of trees.

Millennium Seed Bank – A partnership, coordinated by Royal Botanic Gardens, Kew, set up in 1996 with the goal of collecting and maintaining seeds from 75,000 species of wild plants (25 per cent of known flora) worldwide by 2020. By June 2015 it had stored seed from 34,000 species and almost two billion seeds. The seeds are stored at -20°C in vast underground vaults.

Mycelium – A network of hyphae (see above), sometimes mat-like, which makes up the body of a fungus. Some fungi also form visible fruit bodies, such as mushrooms and brackets, which consist of a modified form of mycelium.

Mycorrhizal fungi – Fungi that form a symbiotic relationship with vascular plants. This relationship is vital for ancient trees' long-term survival. The fungi greatly enhance the function of the roots in absorbing minerals and water from the soil, by virtue of their very extensive network of hyphae. The hyphae are linked to the fine roots of the tree, thus providing the tree with minerals and water, which are then transported to the leaves. By photosynthesis, the leaves produce complex carbohydrates that both the tree and the fungus need for their growth. Fungi are unable to make their own carbohydrates, as they do not possess chlorophyll. So, the mycorrhizal fungus absorbs these nutrients from the roots of the tree in a truly symbiotic relationship. Mycorrhizal fungi also act as a defence barrier fighting off pathogens that try to enter the tree through its fine roots..

Native species – In Great Britain, any species that has occurred naturally since the last Ice Age (see **Exotic trees**).

Palmate – In botany this term refers to leaves with more than three distinct leaflets that radiate from a common point, for example, those of the horse chestnut (*Aesculus hippocastanum*). The term does not apply to species like sycamore (*Acer pseudoplatanus*) or field maple (*Acer campestre*), which have 'lobed' leaves, rather than distinct leaflets.

Pannage – The historic commoners' right to feed pigs or other animals within a forest. Pigs in particular love eating both beech and oak mast (the seeds from these trees).

Pathogens – Organisms, often bacteria, fungi or viruses, which cause infection or disease.

Petroglyphs – Rock carvings or drawings, usually made by prehistoric peoples.

Photosynthesis – The process by which green plants use chlorophyll to produce sugar from carbon dioxide and water using energy from sunlight. Oxygen is generated as a by-product.

Pinnate – In botany this refers to leaves that resemble a feather with parts arranged in the same pattern on both sides of a common axis.

Pollarding – A very old tree management system whereby part or all of the crown of a young tree is removed, encouraging many new branches to grow. This is usually done at approximately 2.5 metres, well above the grazing height of cattle and deer. The new branches are then removed on a rotation based on the desired size. This ranges from five to 30 years. Pollard trees are found in royal hunting forests, wood pastures and within open fields. The advantage of this system is that it provides grazing, as well as wood for building, heating and tools (see also **Wood hay**).

Red Data Book – The IUCN Red List is the world's most comprehensive inventory of species under threat using very strict criteria as laid down by the International Union for the Conservation of Nature. Regional Red Lists (*Red Data Books*) are produced by individual countries when assessing species at risk of extinction.

Retrenchment – The natural process that occurs as trees go into ancientness, also referred to as 'growing down'. Trees put on roughly the same amount of annual growth on their trunks for as long as they can maintain their mature crown-size but, as they get older, this band of annual growth gets narrower and narrower as it is stretched around an ever-increasing girth. In broadleaved species, this leaves less room for the largest-diameter vessels that are the most efficient at transporting water and minerals. Eventually, not enough nutrients can reach the top of the tree. As a result, the crown slowly dies back, which in turn allows more light to reach the lower branches and trunk. The increased light stimulates dormant or new buds to grow and the tree begins forming a new smaller and lower crown, which the vascular network is more capable of supporting. This process can produce a very squat sturdy structure, which is then able to withstand the most extreme winds. Healthy ancient trees with such a shape rarely blow over in storms.

Saproxylic invertebrates – Insects that are dependent on decaying wood for all or part of their lives, or on other insects that are dependent on decaying wood. Often the larvae of these insects feed on decaying wood and the adults feed on other things such as nectar from flowering trees, including hawthorn (*Crataegus*).

Semi-natural woodland – A woodland with a range of plants associated with ancient woodlands. Such a woodland takes many hundreds of years to develop, producing a flora and fauna similar to a natural woodland. There is no truly natural woodland left in Britain or virtually anywhere in Europe, as from the Neolithic period onwards man has managed woodlands, clearing areas by felling trees and shrubs, favouring one species over another, putting domesticated animals to graze, introducing non-native species and killing off the large and dangerous mammals, such as wolves, boar and bears.

SSSI – Sites of Special Scientific Interest are places designated by each devolved government's nature conservation department as being of national importance for a specific species or community of species.

Transpiration – Trees transpire moisture through small pores, or stomata, in their leaves. This process is essential as it allows the tree to draw water and mineral nutrients up from its roots through its vascular network to the leaves by capillary attraction. It is estimated that a large mature oak transpires about 40,000 gallons of water each year.

Umbriferous – Making or providing shade.

Veteran tree – A tree with habitat characteristics similar to those of an ancient tree; so all ancient trees are veteran, but not all veteran trees are ancient.

Veteranisation – The process of deliberately causing physical damage to young and mature trees so as to artificially create veteran features associated with ancient trees. This is recommended when there is a significant age gap between ancient trees and the successor trees that will eventually be able to provide the specialist habitat afforded by ancient trees. Essentially, it involves damaging the tree to expose wood to the decay process, which may include ripping branches from the crown with winches, removing large patches of bark from the tree's trunk or boring holes into the tree to simulate woodpecker holes. This practice may actually shorten the life of the tree but can be vital to maintain continuity for the decaying wood community of fungi and invertebrates.

Wildwood – The term used to describe the original forests across all of Europe before humans 'tamed' it. Historically, it was believed to have been dense impenetrable woodland, but there is growing evidence that it was actually more like a medieval hunting forest: a mosaic of scattered open-grown trees within grassland, areas of thorny scrub and dense woodland. This would have been a dynamic ever-changing ecosystem.

Wood hay – Fodder material collected from the young branches of trees during summer and stored under cover until winter. This was common practice in northern and upland countries across Europe, including Sweden, northern Spain and Switzerland, utilising material from a range of local tree species. This was necessary in these locations with short summers where producing traditional hay was not dependable and the harsh conditions meant there was no grass available for grazing. In Britain, ash and holly were two species commonly used as they are high in protein and favoured by stock.

Bibliography

Baines, E. *The History of the County of Palatine and Duchy of Lancaster*, 1353, vol. 1 (Manchester, 1868).

Bloom, H (ed.). *Bloom's Major Poets: Homer* (New York, 2001).

Bridgeman, P. *Tree Surgery: The Complete Guide* (London, 1977).

Brock, P. 'The old yew and Crom Castle, County Fermanagh', *Irish Gardening*, vol. 3 (Dublin, 1908).

Boulton, H.E. (ed.). *The Sherwood Forest Book* (Thoroton Society, Record Series, vol. XXIII, 1965).

Brydone, P. *A Tour through Sicily and Malta, in a Series of Letters to William Beckford, Esq. of Somerley in Suffolk; from P. Brydone, F.R.S.*, 2 vols (Malta, 1773).

Bullock, S. *After Sixty Years* (London, 1929).

Carroll, L. *Through the Looking-glass And What Alice found there* (London, 1872), chapter 1.

Cheffings, C. and L. Farrell (eds). *The Vascular Plant Red Data List for Great Britain* (Peterborough, 2005).

Chute, F. *The Chutes of The Vyne* (Bognor Regis, 2005).

Clarke, G. 'Where did all the trees come from? An analysis of Bridgeman's planting at Stowe', *Journal of Garden History*, vol. 5, no. 1 (1985).

Day, A. and P. McWilliams (eds). 'Ordnance Survey Memoirs of Ireland Vol. 4, Parishes of County Fermanagh I 1834–5, Enniskillen and Upper Lough Erne', *The Institute of Irish Studies in association with the Royal Irish Academy* (1990).

Deakin, R. *Wildwood: A Journey through Trees* (London, 2016).

Elledge, P. *Lord Byron at Harrow School Speaking Out, Talking Back, Acting Up, Bowing Out* (Baltimore, MD, 2000).

Evelyn, J. *Silva: on a Discourse of Forest-Trees and the Propagation of Timber* (London, 1725).

Evelyn, J. *Diary and correspondence of John Evelyn, F.R.S. To which is subjoined the private correspondence between King Charles I. and Sir Edward Nicholas, and between Sir Edward Hyde, afterwards earl of Clarendon, and Sir Richard Browne* (London, 1850).

Forrest, A. 'Painter in the Park: George Quinton: A series of watercolours revealing Ickworth's "in-between years"', in *National Trust Arts, Buildings and Collections Bulletin* (ABC Bulletin) (Spring 2014).

Greville, M. 'Trees of the royal forest', *Country Life* (3 June 1949).

Grieve, Mrs M. *A Modern Herbal, in two volumes, Volume II: I-Z and Indexes* (London, 1931).

Hageneder, F. *The Living Wisdom of Trees* (London, 2005).

Hageneder, F. *Yew: A History* (Stroud, 2007).

Hall, A.R. *Isaac Newton: Eighteenth-Century Perspectives* (Oxford, New York and Tokyo, 1999).

Hooke, D. *Trees in Anglo-Saxon England: Literature, Lore and Landscape* (Woodbridge, 2010).

King, C.S. (ed.). *Henry's Upper Lough Erne in 1739* (Dublin, 1892).

Knight, C. *et al. The Land We Live In: A Pictorial and Literary Sketch-book of the British Empire*, 4 vols (London, 1847–51).

Lockwood, D. *Francis Kilvert: Borderlines* (Bridgend, 1990).

Lonsdale, D. *Hazards from Trees: A General Guide* (Practice Guide) (Edinburgh, 2000).

Lonsdale, D. (ed.). *Ancient and Other Veteran Trees: Further Guidance on Management* (London, 2014).

Loudon, J.C. *Arboretum et Fruticetum Britannicum*, 8 vols (London, 1838).

Lovasi, G., J. Quinn, K. Neckerman, M. Perzanowski and A. Rundle. 'Children living in areas with more street trees have lower prevalence of asthma', *Journal of Epidemiology & Community Health*, vol. 62, no. 7 (2008).

Lowe, J. *The Yew Trees of Great Britain and Ireland* (London, 1897).

Marchand, L.A. (ed.). *Byron's Letters and Journals* (London, 1976).

Merrett, C. *Pinax rerum naturalium Britannicarum: continens vegetabilia, animalia, et fossilia, in hac insula reperta inchoatus typis* (London, 1666).

Miles, D.W.H. *The Tree-ring Dating of Mottisfont Abbey, Romsey, Hampshire*, Report 23/96 (Ancient Monuments Lab., 1996).

Miles, D. *The Tribes of Britain* (London, 2006).

Morrison, S. 'The creation of Clumber Park, 1709–14: The last royal park of Sherwood Forest', *Trans. Thoroton Society Nottinghamshire*, vol.106 (2002).

O'Brien, S. *In the Footsteps of Augustine Henry* (Suffolk, 2011).

O'Meara, Dr B. *The Opinions and Reflections of Napoleon* (Philadelphia, 1822).

Parker, E. and A. Lewington. *Ancient Trees: Trees That Live for a Thousand Years* (London, 2012).

Pennant, T. *A Tour in Scotland 1769 and a Voyage to the Hebrides* (London, 1772).

Pigott, D. *Lime* (Rye, 2005).

Plover, W. (ed.). *Kilvert's Diary, 1870–79. Selections from the Diary of the Rev. Francis Kilvert* (London, 1964).

Rackham, O. *Trees and Woodland in the British Landscape* (London, 1976).

Rackham, O. *Ancient Woodland: Its History, Vegetation and Use in England* (Cambridge, 1980).

Rackham, O. *The Last Forest: Story of Hatfield Forest* (London, 1993).

Rackham, O. *The Illustrated History of the Countryside* (London, 1997).

Rackham, O. *Woodlands* (London, 2006).

Robinson, E. and G. Summerfield (eds). *Selected Poems and Prose of John Clare* (Cambridge, 1966).

Rotherham, I.D. 'The ecology and economics of medieval deer parks', *Landscape Archaeology and Ecology*, vol. 6 (2007).

Salmon, N. *The History and Antiquities of Essex* (London, 1740).

Strutt, J.G. *Sylva Britannica* or, *Portraits of Forest Trees, Distinguished for their Antiquity, Magnitude, or Beauty* (London, 1830).

Stukeley, W. *Memoirs of Sir Isaac Newton's Life* (London, 1752).

Sylvan. *Sylvan's Pictorial Handbook* (London, 1847).

Tattersfield, N. *John Bewick: Engraver on Wood, 1760–1795: An Appreciation of His Life Together with an Annotated Catalogue of His Illustrations and Designs* (London and New Castle, Delaware, 2010).

Taylor, K. 'The development of the park and gardens at Knole', *Archaeologia Cantiana*, vol. 123 (2003).
'The biggest oaks in Britain: famous trees at Powis Castle', *Country Life* (22 June 1935).
Tyers, I. *Tree-ring Analysis of the Roof of the Samwell Wing at Felbrigg Hall, Felbrigg, Norfolk*, Report 65/98 (Ancient Monuments Lab., 1998).
Ulrich, R.S. 'View through a window may influence recovery from GP practice', *Science*, vol. 224 (1984).
Vera, F.W.M. *Grazing Ecology and Forest History* (Wallingford, 2000).
Waterson, M. 'Woods and Woodmen of Erddig', *Country Life* (5 October 1978), pp. 1034, 1036.
Wordsworth, W. *The Collected Poems of William Wordsworth* (Ware, 1994).
Young, A. *General View of the Agriculture of the County of Essex 2* (Essex, 1807).
Young, Revd A. 'Observations registered in the course of a visit to the Right Hon. the Earl of Coventry, at Croome, Worcestershire', *Annals of Agriculture and Other Useful Arts*, vol. 37 (October 2012).

Picture Credits

All images © National Trust/Edward Parker except:

pp. 8, 9 (below), 10 (below), 13 (above and below), 14, 15, 125 (below): Brian Muelaner; p. 11: National Trust/John Shipperbotthom; p. 20: National Trust/Westair Publishing; p. 24: National Trust/Michael Caldwell; pp. 26, p. 115 (below), 120 (above): National Trust/Andrew Butler; pp. 36, 129 (above): National Trust/David Cousins; p. 39: National Trust/Nick Meers; pp. 46, 52 (above), 58 (above), 62 (below), 106 (left and right): National Trust; p. 51: National Trust Images/NaturePL/Alan Williams; pp. 56, 57 (below): National Trust Images/Chris Lacey; p. 57 (above): © National Museums Northern Ireland, Collection Ulster Museum, BELUM.Y13846; p. 61 (above): Andrew Butler; p. 61 (below): National Museum of Wales, NLW MS20143A, fol. 39r; p. 63 (below): National Trust Images/Andrew Butler; p. 65 (above): National Trust/Angelo Hornak; p. 67 (left): © blickwinkel/Alamy Stock Photo; p. 68: Harvard University Library – Arnold Arboretum Horticultural Library, AAE-02776; p. 70 (below): National Trust Images/NaturePL/David Kjaer; p. 72 (above): National Trust Images; pp. 75 (below), 109, 126 (above): National Trust/John Miller; p. 77 (below): Edward Parker, photographed from Strutt 1830; p. 82: National Trust/Joe Cornish; p. 83: Roger Clegg; p. 89 (below): from Young 1807, plate 45, Essex Record Office; p. 91: FLPA/Alamy Stock Photo; p. 92: National Trust/Ray Dale; p. 96 (below): © North Wind Picture Archives/Alamy Stock Photo; p. 101: National Trust Images/Stephen Robson; p. 102: National Trust/Chris Lacey; p. 103 (below): © SOTK2011/Alamy Stock Photo; p. 105 (above): National Trust/John Hammond; pp. 107, 117 (above), 143, 150: National Trust/Robert Morris; p. 113: Courtesy of Sir Richard Hyde Parker, DL. Photo: Edward Parker; p. 114 (right): National Trust Images/NaturePL/Gary K. Smith; p. 122 (above): © Tate, London 2015; p. 141 (left): National Trust Images/NaturePL/Colin Seddon; p. 149 (below): The Royal Society, RS.9417; back flap of book jacket: portrait of Edward Parker: Jay Griffiths; portrait of Brian Muelaner: National Trust/Brian Clecker.

Index

arrows, ash 36
ash (*Fraxinus excelsior*)
  animal feed 36
  cropping 32–33, *32*
  Dinefwr, Carmarthenshire *62*, 63
  diseased 133–34, *133*
  faggots 36, *36*
  Felbrigg, Norfolk 70
  Kedleston Hall, Derbyshire 98
  Stourhead, Wiltshire 128
Ashridge Estate, Hertfordshire 23–25
aspen, common (*Populus tremula*) 120
avenues, tree
  beech 105, 109
  elm 114
  lime 46, 64, 81, 118, 133, 143
  oak 114
  Studley Royal 81
  sweet chestnut 51, 52, 129–30
azalea (*Azalea*) 73, 109, 128

Badbury Rings (earthwork) 104
Bankes, William John 104–105
Barker-Mill, Revd John 118
bats 60, 109, 139, *141*
beech (*Fagus sylvatica*)
  'Bundle Beech' 44, *44*
  Dunham Massey, Cheshire 64, *64*
  Felbrigg, Norfolk 70
  Frithsden Woods, Ashridge Estate 23–25, *23*
  'King Beech' 106
  Kingston Lacy, Dorset 104, *104–105*
  Lanhydrock, Cornwall 109–10
  Plas Newydd, Anglesey 124–25, *124*
  Stourhead, Wiltshire 128
beech, southern (*Nothofagus*) 120, *122*, 146
beetles
  click (*sp. Elateridae*) 99
  cobweb (*Ctesias serra*) 39
  darkling (*Pseudocistela ceramboides*) 65, *67*
  death-watch (*Xestobium rufovillosum*) 99
  dung (*Scarabidae*) 140
  false darkling (*Abdera quadrifasciata*) 65
  flat bark (*Pediacus depressus*) 65
  hister (*Aeletes atomarius*) 65
  species 39, 64
  stag (*Lucanus cervus*) 98
biodiversity 47, 99, 110, 113
birch (*Betula*) 8, 103, *103*, 138

Blickling, Norfolk 26–27, *26–27*
bluebells (*Hyacinthoides non-scripta*) 26
Bonaparte, Napoleon 118
Borrowdale, Cumbria *12*, 28–33, *28*
box (*Buxus sempervirens*) 34
Box Hill, Surrey 34–35, *34–35*
bramble (*Rubus fruticosus*) 92
Branscombe, Devon 36–37, *36*, *37*
Bridgeman, Charles 133
Brocas Jnr, Henry 56
Brock, Peter 56–57
Brown, Capability 58, *58*, 60, 73, 120, 122–23, 129, 133
Bullock, Shan 56
butterflies *115*
Byron, Lord 105

Calke Abbey, Derbyshire 39–43, *39*
cattle 15, 61, *61*, *86–87*
Caux, Maud de 46
cedar, Deodar (*Cedrus deodara*) 103
cedar of Lebanon (*Cedrus libani*) *58*, 60, 96–97, *96–97*
charcoal 47
cherries, oriental (*Acer*) 128
cherry, wild (*Prunus avium*) *80–81*, 81
chestnut, horse (*Aesculus hippocastanum*) *90*, 91, *99*, 128
chestnut, sweet (*Castanea sativa*)
  Croft Castle, Hertfordshire 50–52, *52*
  Dunham Massey, Cheshire 64
  Felbrigg, Norfolk 70
  Kingston Lacy, Dorset 105
  Mottisfont Abbey, Hampshire 117
  Petworth House and Park, West Sussex *8*, 122
  Petworth Park, West Sussex 123
  Sicilian example 52
  Stourhead, Wiltshire *6*, 129–30, *130*
  Studley Royal *78–79*, 80–81
China, specimens from 68
Chirk, Wales *15*
Church of St Mary, Studley Royal *80*, 81
Chute, Chaloner 143
Chute, William John 143
Chute, William Lyde Wiggett 143
Cistercian monks 76
Clare, John 137
climate change 26, 48, 83, 125
Clumber Park, Nottinghamshire 44–46, *45*, *46*

Cole, William 75
Collier family *36*
commemorations, trees as 46, 109
Conduitt, John 148
Coniston Water, Cumbria *10*, 47–49, *47–49*
coppicing 11, *11*, 70, *120*
Cordell, William 113
Cove, Bill 39
Coventry, George William, 6th Earl of Coventry 58, 60
Croft Castle, Hertfordshire *10*, *17*, 50–55, *52*, *54–55*
Crom Estate, County Fermanagh 56–57, *56*
Croome Park, Worcestershire 58–60, *58*, *60*
Crow, James 120
cypress (*Cupressus*) 58, 129

David, Father Armand 68
Dda, King Hywel 61
Deakin, Roger 36
deer
  fallow (*Dama dama*) *63*, *64*, 120
  red (*Cervus elaphus*) 80
  sika (*Cervus nippon*) 80
deer parks
  Dinefwr, Carmarthenshire 61–62
  Dunham Massey, Cheshire 64, *66*
  Felbrigg, Norfolk 70
  Ickworth Park, Suffolk 92, *93*
  Kedleston Hall, Derbyshire 98–99
  Knole, Kent 106–107
  Petworth House and Park, West Sussex 120, *122*
  Studley Royal 80–81, *81*
  Vyne Estate, Hampshire 143
Dinefwr, Carmarthenshire 61–63, *61*, *62*, *63*
diseases 51, 91, 133–34, 141, *141*, 151
Disraeli, Benjamin, 1st Earl of Beaconsfield 91
DNA testing 32
dog's mercury plant (*Mercurialis perennis*) 26
Dolbury Hill ('Clump') 100, 103
Domesday book 46, 70, 92, 134
dove-tree (*Davidia involucrata*) 68
Drake, Sir Francis 50
Dunham Massey, Cheshire 64–67, *64*, 65

Egyptians 77
elder (*Sambucus nigra*) *133*, 134
elm (*Ulmus*) 76, 114

Elysian Fields 133
Emmetts Garden, Kent 68–69, *69*
Enclosure Acts 113, 136–37
Evelyn, John 34, 51

Felbrigg, Norfolk 70–72, *71*
FitzStephen, Ralph 46
Florence Court, County Fermanagh 74–75, *74–75*
flycatchers, spotted (*Muscicapa striata*) 139
Fountains Abbey, North Yorkshire 76, *76*
'Fraternal Four' yews (Borrowdale) 29–32, *29–31*
Frith, Francis 106
Frithsden Woods, Ashridge Estate 23–25, *23*, *24*, *151*
fungi
  beefsteak (*Fistulina hepatica*) *9*, 99
  big blue pinkgill (*Entoloma bloxamii*) 138
  chicken of the woods (*Lactiporus sulphureus*) 99
  common southern bracket (*Ganoderma australe*) 99
  date-coloured waxcap (*Hygrocybe spadicea*) 138
  decay 81, 120, 122
  Dinefwr, Carmarthenshire 62
  giant polypore (*Meripilus giganteus*) 64, *64*
  mushrooms 47
  mycorrhizal 14–15, 16
  oak polypore (*Piptoporus quercinus*) 99
  pink waxcap (*Hygrocybe calyptriformis*) 138

gardens, National Trust 16
Gifford, Lady Anne 106
Glenamara Park 138
Glencoyne Farm 138, 141
gnat, fungus (*Scythropochroa quercicola*) 65
Gowbarrow Fell, Cumbria *139–40*
Gowbarrow Park 138, 141
graffiti 25, *25*, 72, *72*
Great Wood, Blickling, Norfolk 26–27
Great Wood, Felbrigg, Norfolk 70–72
Green, Ted 83
Greville, Maynard 89
Grieve, Maud 49

Hadrian's Wall Estate, Northumberland 82–83, *82*
handkerchief trees (*Davidia involucrata*) 68, *69*
Harpur-Crewe, Vauncey, 10th Baronet 42
Harpur family 39
Hatfield Forest, Essex 84–89, *84–87*
hawthorn (*Crataegus monogyna*) 53, 92, 103, *103*
health benefits, of trees 91, 115, 149
Henry, Augustine 68
Henry, Dr William Henry, Dean of Killaloe 56
Henry VIII, King 113, 117, 120, 143, 144
herons (*Ardea cinerea*) 114
Hoare, Henry II 128, 130
Hoare, Richard Colt 128
Holles, John, 1st Duke of Newcastle 44
Holt Forest *13*
hornbeam (*Carpinus betulus*)
  Hatfield Forest, Essex 84, *85*, *88–89*
  Scotney Castle, Kent 126, *126–27*
  Vyne Estate, Hampshire 143, *145*
horses *46*, 64, 65, 91, 98
hoverflies 49
Howard family 141
Hughenden, Buckinghamshire 90–91, *90*
Huguenots 112
hunting 84–89, 112, 120
Hyde Parker family 111, 113
Hyde Parker, Sir Richard 113

'Ice Man' (Özi) 35
Ickworth Park, Suffolk 92–96, *92–97*, *96*
invertebrates, saproxylic 6, 9, 60, 62, 98, 134
Iron Age 83, 104
ivy (*Hedera*) *9*

Jackson, Andy 146
James I, King 111
John, Earl of Morton 46
Johnson, Boris 115

Kedleston Hall, Derbyshire *18–19*, 98–99, *98–99*
Kent, William 133
Killerton, Devon 100–103, *102*
Kilvert, Frances 52
kingfishers (*Alcedo atthis*) 114, *114*
Kingston Lacy, Dorset 104–105, *105*
Knole, Kent 106–107, *107*

Lake District 33, 47–49, 138–41
land management 11–16, *11–12*
landscape designers 72, 98, 100, 133, 143
Lanhydrock, Cornwall *9*, 108–10, *109*, *110*
Laws of Hywel Dda (Welsh text) *61*
lichen 9, 53, 70, 109, 139, *140*, 141
lime, common (*Tilia x Europaea*) *45*
lime, hybrid (*Tilia*) 42, *80*, 81
lime, large-leaved (*Tilia platyphyllos*) 34–35, *35*
lime, small-leaved (*Tilia cordata*)
  Borrowdale, Cumbria 33
  Calke Abbey, Derbyshire 39, *40–41*
  Coniston Water, Cumbria *48*, *49*
  Hatfield Forest, Essex 84
  Petworth Park, West Sussex *120*, 122
  'walking' 26–27, *27*, 39, *43*, 48
Loder, Gerald 146
longbows, yew 20–22, *22*, 36
Loudon, John Claudius 89
Lowe, John 32
Lowe, Sir Hudson 118
Lyminge, Robert 26

Magna Carta (1215) 20, *20*
maple (*Acer campestre*) 82, *84*, 128, 146
Medlar (*Mespilus germanica*) 53
Melford Hall, Suffolk *14*, 111–13, *111*, *113*
Meredith, Allan 77
Merrett, Christopher 34
Mill family (Mottisfont) 117
Millennium Seed Bank 146, 151
Moccas Park 52
Moir, Dr Andy 146
Morden Hall Park, London 114–15, *115*
Mosaic Mapping 8
moths, leaf-mining (*Cameraria ohridella*) 91, *91*
Mottisfont Abbey, Hampshire 116–19, *117*
mulberry
  black (*Morus nigra*) 111–12, *111*, 114, *114*
  white (*Morus alba*) 111–12
mushrooms 47
mythology 49, 63, 73, 107, 133

National Nature Reserve (NNR) 39, 61
Natural England (English nature) Species Recovery Project 110
Newton, Sir Isaac 148
North Downs 35

oak, English (*Quercus robur*)
  Beelzebub 120
  'Oakley Oak' (Mottisfont) 117, *117*
  Stourhead, Wiltshire 129
  'Tea Party Oak' *2*, 92–96, *93*, *96*
oak (*Quercus*)
  Croft Castle, Hertfordshire *10*
  Croome Park, Worcestershire 60, *60*
  'Damory Oak,' Dorset 89
  'Doodle Oak,' Hatfield Forest 89, *89*
  Dunham Massey, Cheshire 64, *66*, *67*
  'Farey Oak' (Stowe, Buckinghamshire) 134, *135*
  Hatfield Forest, Essex 84
  holly/holm (*Quercus ilex*) 105
  'Hundred Guinea Oak' *142*, 143–44, *144*
  Ickworth Park, Suffolk *94–95*
  Kedleston Hall, Derbyshire 98, *99*
  Killerton, Devon *100*
  'King John Oak' (Knole, Kent) 106
  Lanhydrock, Cornwall *108*, 110
  in literature 107
  Melford Hall, Suffolk 112, *112*
  Morden Hall Park, London 114
  Mottisfont Abbey, Hampshire 117
  Old Man of Calke 9, 39, *42*
  'Old Oak' (Knole, Kent) 106, *106*
  Petworth Park, West Sussex *121*
  Plas Newydd, Anglesey 124, *125*
  Quarry (*Quercus petraea*) *50*, 52–53
  sheep grazing *18–19*
  and shipbuilding 144
  Studley Royal 80, *81*
  Vyne Estate, Hampshire 143
oak, sessile (*Quercus petraea*) *9*, *71*, 72, 106, 120
O'Meara, Dr Barry 118
orchards 53, 149
Orlando (Woolf) 107

pannage 23
pear, Plymouth (*Pyrus cordata*) 110, *110*
Pelham-Clinton, Henry, 4th Duke of Newcastle 46
Pennant, Thomas 33
Petworth House and Park, West Sussex *8*, 120–23, *120*, *122*
Pierse, Samuel 112
pigs 23–25, 51
pine, Scots (*Pinus sylvestris*) 73
plane
  London (*Platanus x acerifolia*) *59*, *116*, 117–18
  North American (*Platanus occidentalis*) 118
  oriental (*Platanus orientalis*) 118
plant collectors 68, *68*, 100, 109
Plas Newydd, Anglesey 124–25
pollarding
  ash *12*, *28*, 33, *33*, *37*, *98*, *140*
  beech *151*
  hawthorn 53, *53*
  hornbeam 126
  maple 84
  oak *13–15*, *54–55*, 60, *92*
  Repton's Pollard 124
  revival 150
  sycamore 136
  'Tea Party Oak' 92
pollen studies 48–49, 83
poplar
  grey (*Populus x canescens*) 120, *123*
  white (*Populus alba*) 120

Rackham, Oliver 64, 84, 92, 113
redstart (*Phoenicurus phoenicurus*) 70, *70*
redwood
  coast (*Sequoia sempervirens*) 129
  dawn (*Metasequoia glyptostroboides*) 129, *131*
  giant (*Sequoiadendron giganteum*) 100–101, *101*, *103*, 129
religion 97
Repton, Sir Humphry 72–73, 123, 124, 129
rhododendron (*Rhododendron*) 73, 109, 128
Richard III, King 22
ring dating (dendrochronology) 146
Robartes, Sir Richard 109
Rock Walk (Wakehurst Place, West Sussex) 146
rowan (*Sorbus aucuparia*) 8
Royal Botanic Gardens, Kew 146
Royal Navy 72, 143, 144
Rysbrack, John Michael 133

Sandys, Sir William of Mottisfont 117, 143
saproxylic invertebrates 6, 9, 60, 62, 98, 134
Scotney Castle, Kent 126–27, *126*
Scots pine (*Pinus sylvestris*) *73*
Second World War 25, *67*, 92, 96
seeds 47–48, 51, 68, 103, 146
sequoia, giant *See* redwood, giant (*Sequoiadendron giganteum*)
'Seven Sisters' (Fountains Abbey) *77*
sheep 12, 15, *18–19*, 33
Sheringham Park, Norfolk 72–73, *72*
Sherwood Forest 44, 46
shipbuilding 72, 143, 144
Shugborough, Shropshire 56
silk industry 111–12
Site of Special Scientific Interest (SSSI) 39, 70
slugs 72
Spanish Armada 51
Spanish chestnut (*Castanea sativa*) *See* sweet chestnut (*Castanea sativa*)
spruce, Sitka (*Picea sitchensis*) *138*, 141
SSSI (Site of Special Scientific Interest) 39, 70
Stourhead, Wiltshire 128–31, *128–29*
Stourton, Barons of 130
Stowe, Buckinghamshire 132–35
Strutt, Jacob George 76, *77*
Stuckley, William 148
Studley Royal Park 80–81, *80–81*
sycamore (*Acer pseudoplatanus*)
  Hadrian's Wall Estate, Northumberland *82–83*
  history of 82–83
  Knole, Kent *107*
  Lanhydrock, Cornwall 109–10
  Plas Newydd, Anglesey *125*
  Repton's Pollard 124
  'Sycamore Gap' 82
  Tolpuddle Martyrs' Tree 136, *137*
  See also maple (*Acer campestre*)
symbolism 49, 73, 77, 134
Syon Park, London 114

Thurstan, Archbishop of York 76
timber, use of
  animal feed 36, 126
  buildings 88, *150*
  fuel 12, 33, 82, 112, 126
  rope-making 35
  sales of 64
  shipbuilding 72, 143, 144
  tools 35, 36, 126
Tolpuddle Martyrs' (commemorative plaque) *136*
Tolpuddle Martyrs' Tree, Dorset 136–37
tree creeper *(Certhia familiaris)* 60
tree management 8, 81, *81*, 113, 124, 150–51

tulip tree (*Liriodendron tulipifera*) 128, 129, *129*
Turner, Joseph Mallord William (J. M. W.) 120, 122–23
Turner, Revd Charles 148

Ullswater, Cumbria 138–41, *139*
Ulrich, Roger 114

Veitch, John 100
Veitch, Sir Harry 68
Vera, Franz 139–40
'veteranisation' 9–10
Victory, HMS 144
Vyne Estate, Hampshire 142–45, *143*

Wakehurst Place, West Sussex 146–47
warblers, wood (*Phylloscopus sibilatrix*) *51*, 70, 139
weather
  gales 13, 32, 106, 125
  'mini Ice Age' 92, 96
  rain 48, 115, 141
  storms *30–31*, 32, *80*, 81, 106, *106*, 143
  sun 13
Webb, John 143
wetlands 62–63, 75, 143
Willis, George 75
willow, corkscrew (*Salix matsudana 'Tortuosa'*) 114
willow (*Salix*) 47, 58, 88, 114, 143
Wilson, Ernest 68, *68*, 129
Winter Solstice 77
wood pasture management 10–14, *17*, *26*, 84, 138–39, *139*, 141, *144*, 150
woodpeckers 60, 138
Woolsthorpe Manor, Lincolnshire 148–49
Wordsworth, William 29, 77
World Heritage Sites 76
Wyatt, James 124

yellow archangel plant (*Lamium galeobdolon*) 26
yew, Irish (*Taxus baccata var. fastigiata*) *74–75*, 75
yew (*Taxus baccata*)
  Ankerwycke Yew 20, *21*
  Box Hill, Surrey *34*
  Crom Estate, County Fermanagh 56–57, *57*
  and longbows 20–22, *22*
  longevity 9
  and religion 77
  'Seven Sisters' (Fountains Abbey) 76–77, *76–77*
  Stowe, Buckinghamshire *134*
  Wakehurst Place, West Sussex 146, *146–47*
  'walking' 133